LANDSCAPE
How to

Real People – Real Projects™

HOMETIME®

Publisher: Dean Johnson
Editor: Pamela S. Price
Writer: John Kelsey
Art Director: Bill Nelson
Photo Editor: Jason Adair
Copy Editor: Lisa Wagner

Hometime Hosts: Dean Johnson, Robin Hartl
Project Producers: Matt Dolph, Wade Barry
Construction and Technical Review: Mark Kimball,
Dan Laabs, Judd Nelson

Illustrator: Mario Ferro
Photographer: Jeff Lyman
Cover Photo: Maki Strunc Photography
Location Photography Manager: Michael Klaers,
Tom (Buki) Weckwerth
Video Frame Capture: Julie Wallace, Jennifer Parks
Photoshop Effects: Steve Burmeister

Production Coordinator: Pam Scheunemann
Electronic Layout: Chris Long

Book Creative Direction, Design and Production:
MacLean & Tuminelly, Minneapolis, MN
Cover Design: Richard Scales Advertising Associates

Library of Congress Catalog Card Number 97-74166
ISBN 1-890257-02-8

H O M E T I M E®
4275 Norex Drive
Chaska, MN 55318

Special Thanks: A to Z Rental; Aquapore Moisture
Systems; Laurie Robinson, Bailey Nursery; Books
That Work; Pam Parker Dunlap; Halla Nursery;
Wells Lamont

Contributing Photography: Bailey Nursery,
California Redwood Association, Indiana Division
of Soil Conservation, Intermatic Malibu, Keystone
Retaining Systems, Lilypons Water Gardens,
Minnesota Extension Service, Portland Cement
Association, Prairie Restoration, Inc.

The work and procedures shown and described in
this book are intended for use by people having
average skills and knowledge of the subjects. If
you are inexperienced in using any of the tools,
equipment, or procedures depicted or described,
or think that the work and procedures shown and
described in this book may not be safe in your
chosen situation, consult a person skilled in the
performance of the work or procedure.
Throughout this book there are specific safety
recommendations. Pay careful attention to each
of these.

    The makers of this book disclaim any liability
for injury or damage arising out of any failure or
omission to perform the work or procedures shown
and described in this book. Your performance is at
your own risk.

5 4 3 2   02 01 00 99 98

Electronic Prepress: Encore Color Group
Printed by: Quebecor Printing

Printed in the United States

*For online project help and information on other
Hometime products, visit us on the Web at*
www.hometime.com

Introduction

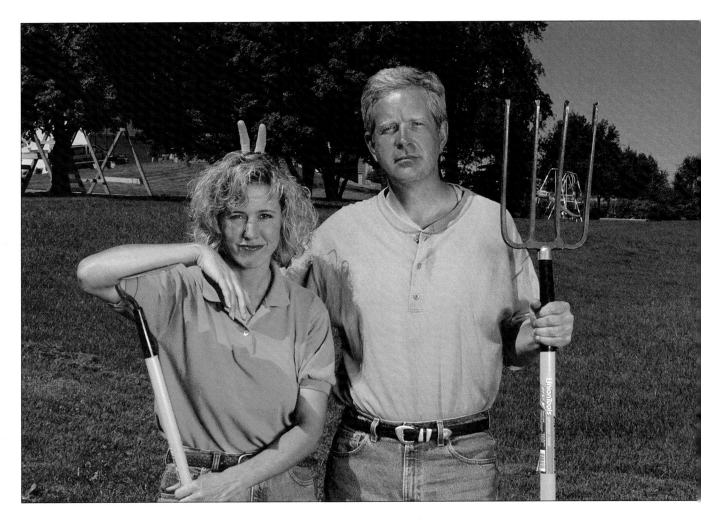

Robin Hartl   *Dean Johnson*

There are a lot of good reasons to take on a landscape project, like: the only thing growing on your lot is your brand new house; you want your yard to reflect your personality, not the previous owner's; if the hill out back erodes any more, you'll soon have an earth-sheltered house.

But perhaps the best reason of all is the bottom line. A good landscape job will add value to your home. Plus, you can do most – if not all – of the work yourself and save a bundle doing it.

We've covered all the basics in this book: planning, grading, drainage, retaining walls, fences, patios, trees, shrubs, and lawns. Read it carefully before you tackle your project; it will help you handle most of the challenges you'll encounter in your landscaping project. However, since each yard is unique, you may run into something we haven't covered. Check out other resources (such as books, videos, the Internet, contractors, landscape suppliers, and local nurseries) for solutions you can adapt to suit your situation.

Work safely and don't spend too many hours under the hot sun. Remember that no landscape is static – you'll never really be done. When that thought seems overwhelming, take the time to sit out on that patio you built, sip a cold drink, and watch the flowers grow. You'll soon find your enthusiasm coming back.

Table of Contents

PLANNING

Before you stick a shovel in the ground, *take the time to make a thorough landscape plan of your entire property. The advantage of having a good plan is that it keeps you from being overwhelmed; a plan will help you break the huge task of landscaping into manageable and affordable stages. Without a plan, it's all too easy to get jobs out of order, so you might find yourself tearing up a newly installed patio to lay the drain you should have put down first. When the job is as big as landscaping your entire property, it always pays to take the time to think it through first.*

Assessing Your Landscaping Needs

Whether you've lived in your home for years or have just moved in, the way to begin landscape planning is to take a good look at what you've got. Make a list of your yard's good and bad points. Then make a list of the improvements you want to make. Supplement your lists with sketches, diagrams, and photographs. While you can organize the planning process in just a few hours, it's best to keep the actual planning going for a full year, so you can chart the effects of the seasons.

You'll find that writing things down makes you really take notice. You'll see aspects of your yard that you hadn't thought about before, good and bad. Look at what your neighbors have done with their yards, too. Sometimes you'll find that the same feature has both positive and negative aspects. For example, the trees that shade the house in summer fill the gutters with leaves in autumn.

Drainage and erosion

To solve a water problem you have to know its source. Surface water runs on top of the ground. If you go out after a rain, you'll see the water and can follow its course. Subsurface water percolates through the soil until it hits a barrier, such as a layer of clay, a rock ledge, or the foundation of the house. A boggy area that never seems to dry or mysterious water in the basement both indicate subsurface water.

Things to think about

Every property is different and every family has its own set of needs. Here's a list of points to consider that will help you start planning your landscaping projects.

Drainage	Decks
Erosion	Sunlight
Irrigation	Winter wind
Privacy	Shade trees
Noise control	Flowering trees
Entrances	Lawns
Walks and steps	Ground covers
Entertaining	Flower gardens
Play spaces	Vegetable gardens
Pet areas	Foundation
Fences	plantings
Walls	Maintenance
Terraces	Curb appeal
Patios	

Landscaping is more than trees and shrubs. It creates outdoor living spaces for your family, and also modifies the climate around your house, directing the sun, wind, and water to your best advantage. Landscaping also makes your home more attractive and inviting, and increases its resale value.

Retaining walls *made of concrete block, stone, or landscaping ties can change eroding hillsides into stable, useful, and attractive terraces and gardens.*

What *do you want from your yard? Every family's needs are different, and will change with time.*

Sometimes the solution is as simple as changing the slope of the land so the water flows away from the house without causing harm. However, you may also need to change the composition of the soil (by adding sand or organic material), so it can absorb water better. And in some situations you'll have to dig trenches and lay drains.

Privacy

Everyone likes to be neighborly, but when the neighbors can watch your every move, it becomes uncomfortable to spend time outdoors. Think of outdoor spaces as extensions of indoor rooms, with fences and plantings for walls. When outdoor rooms are private, they generally get more use. The spaces where you spend the most time, such as the deck or patio, are where privacy matters the most.

Privacy screens work two ways. They allow you to control what can be seen from outside the yard. They also allow you to screen out unpleasant views, such as busy traffic or commercial installations. It's also important to screen sound. You don't want to hear the noise of the street, and you probably don't want to broadcast your conversations.

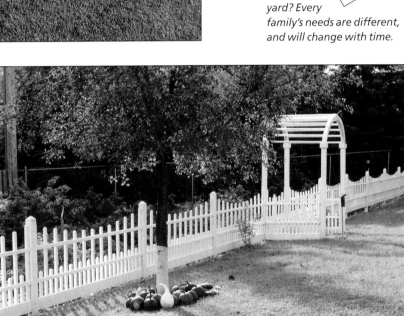

Curb appeal

Most people want their home to look good and express a bit of individuality. Curb appeal is more than plants and trees, driveways and walkways, though. It's how you fit these elements together that makes your home appealing. It's also a long-term proposition, because no landscape is static. Materials weather and plants change with the seasons.

When it comes time to sell the house, curb appeal is important. Potential buyers will make their decision within seconds of driving up to your house, based entirely on curb appeal.

A fence *can contain just a portion of the yard. This picket fence protects a garden from people and some animals. Plans for the arbor are on page 73.*

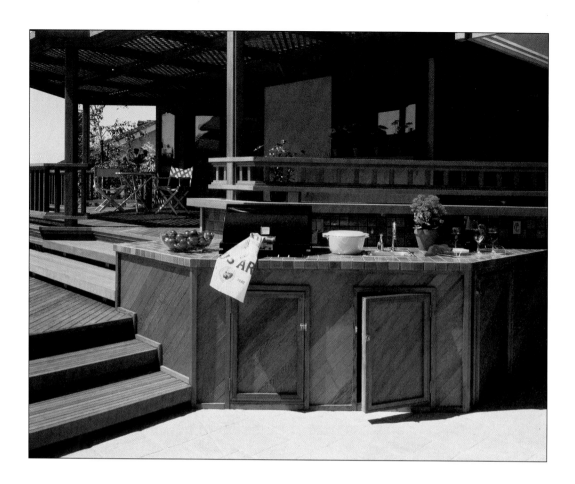

Outdoor rooms provide space for open-air dining, entertaining, and relaxing.

What's Important in Your Landscape?

Outdoor activities generally require four different kinds of space; each will be present in almost any landscaping plan. These categories are social spaces such as patios and decks; gardening spaces for flowers, vegetables, and ornamental plants; play space for children, pets, and adults; and utility zones for driveways, tool storage, and maintenance access.

Think about what matters to you. Some people don't mind storing their gardening tools in the garage, but a serious gardener probably wants a separate shed with workspace as well as storage. Woodworkers and artists often want to put up separate studios or workshops, which may also need driveway access. Home auto mechanics may want to build a second garage with a grease pit.

Social spaces

Everyone loves outdoor living and it's usually obvious where to do it: near the house, and away from the street. But how you organize your outdoor spaces depends on your family's needs and lifestyle, as well as your lot and its topography. You might prefer to have one large lawn for parties, but your sloping site may force you to create a number of smaller terraces and outdoor rooms.

For outdoor dining, most people prefer the hard surface of a patio or deck, which should be close to the indoor kitchen so it's easy to transport food and dishes. Also consider the effect of the sun on your dining area. Early morning warmth will enhance outdoor breakfasts, but early evening sun may be too intense for dining. For outdoor lunches, you'll probably need the shade of a leafy tree, a pergola, or an awning.

For outdoor parties, choose the space closest to your indoor entertainment rooms, so the crowd can move easily between the house, deck, and garden. An outdoor spa probably should be accessible to the master bedroom, as well as to the deck.

Gardening spaces

Vegetable and flower gardens need to be on level ground, on terraces, or in raised beds. Most people place vegetable gardens in the backyard, while a flower garden is appropriate almost anywhere, as is a mixed garden of vegetables and herbs. Locate gardens so there's easy access for you and your tools.

Use ornamental plantings, shrubs, and trees to define the different spaces in your landscape. A row of shrubs can make a backdrop for flowering plants. A low hedge or a row of perennials can divide the play area from the patio. A hedge of evergreen shrubs creates the same sense of privacy as a tall fence.

Play spaces

If you have little kids, you'll want their sandbox and climbing structure to be near the house so you can keep an eye on them. Older children have more toys and equipment, they make more noise, and they need more space, but they don't require such close supervision. Their playground can be a little farther from the house.

Utility zones

The driveway is the principal means of access to your property. If you entertain frequently, or keep a home office, you may want to enlarge your driveway to provide off-street parking. A boat or a camper may also need its own parking space. If your property is large, you

When a vegetable garden is high on your list of priorities, you'll want to pick a spot with at least six hours of full sun, though most people wouldn't locate it in the front yard.

might want to extend a service spur from your main driveway for maintenance vehicles.

Sidewalks, walkways, and footpaths make the connections between the various parts of your landscape. Make sure your pathways are wide enough for wheelchairs, garden carts, and lawnmowers, consider ramps instead of steps, and make sure you don't inadvertently force all the maintenance equipment to roll through your outdoor dining area. If your home has no front walk besides the driveway, consider creating one. Separate access for people on foot is a comfortable amenity that's often missing from today's subdivision.

A flower garden brings color, beauty, and pleasure to any landscape. You can choose annuals and perennials for a continuous show of blooms from spring through early fall.

Ground cover	Lawn grass

Annual flowers	Perennial flowers

Vegetables	Hedge

Deciduous trees, shrubs — Evergreen trees, shrubs

Brick pavers — Concrete pavers

Wood decking — Fence

Landscape architects have a language of symbols for plan views. They save a lot of time, and help you communicate clearly with your suppliers.

Drawing a Site Map

To plan where you want to go, you need an accurate map of where you are now. Start with the real estate survey of your property. A survey map will show the lot lines, the buildings, and perhaps the driveway, but it's not likely to show anything about the lay of the land, or the location of trees and shrubs. Make several copies of the site map. If it's not in ⅛-inch scale (the usual scale for landscape plans), reduce or enlarge it on a photocopier.

Starting from known features, like the house and the street, use a 100-foot tape to measure the location of existing fences, walls, sidewalks, trees, shrubs, patios, decks, driveways, and gardens. Use a compass and the ⅛-inch scale on an architect's rule to transfer the measurements to your site plan. Note the location of doorways, downspouts, drains, electrical wires, and other utilities.

Next, add some notes about the slope, or grade, of the land. To measure elevations and slopes you can rent a transit and rod or a laser transit, but the simplest way is to tape a level to the edge of a straight 8-foot stud. Using the leveled stud and a tape measure, you can directly measure slopes and drops. It's slow going, but accurate enough.

Finally, make a single ⅛-inch scale drawing of your entire property. To help you develop your ideas in more detail, make ¼-inch scale drawings of each area where you intend to make major changes.

Lay tracing paper over a photo and sketch how your house will look once the trees grow and other plantings mature.

Landscape planning

Now it's time to start filtering all your good ideas onto your site plan. Be sure you work on copies (not on the original), so you can try out different ideas. Along with your wish list and your site plan, you've probably got a stack of magazine articles and catalog photos showing things you'd like to have in your landscape. Visit local nurseries, too. You'll usually find the staff has practical information about what works – and what doesn't – in your area.

Most people have trouble visualizing a plan in three dimensions. One good way to think through your ideas is to take photographs of your yard from various viewpoints, enlarge them on a color photocopier, and lay drafting vellum or tracing paper over top. Then sketch your ideas on the tracing paper.

Be sure to sketch trees and shrubs at their mature sizes so you don't overplant. The young plants will look sparse at first, so plan to fill in with annuals for the first couple of years.

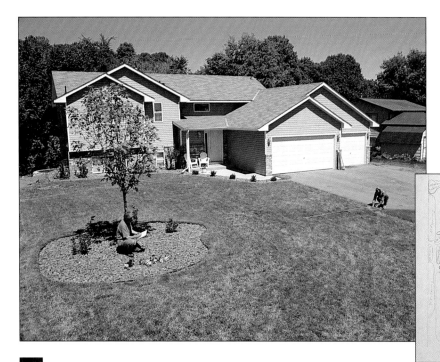

Sketch in all important features and activity areas on your landscape plan. Don't worry about detail yet, just draw circles. Landscapers call this a bubble plan.

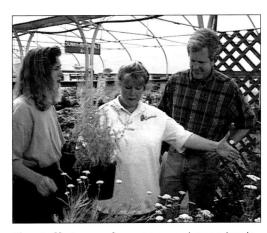

The staff at a good nursery can give you invaluable information about which trees and shrubs will thrive in your climate. Go on a quiet morning and take your site plan with you.

3-D computer design programs take you on a virtual walk-through of your plan. Look for software with a large plant library and the ability to show growth habits and seasonal changes.

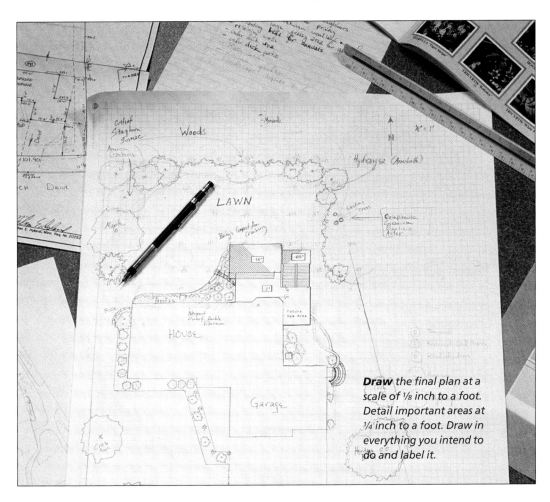

Draw the final plan at a scale of 1/8 inch to a foot. Detail important areas at 1/4 inch to a foot. Draw in everything you intend to do and label it.

Underground sprinklers

If you decide to install an underground sprinkler system, you'll be able to say good-bye to tangled hoses and vacation-parched lawns. However, the whole system should be planned before you lay any pipe, because you have to make sure there'll be enough water pressure.

The total flow in each sprinkler circuit shouldn't exceed 60% of the available water pressure. Your sprinkler dealer should be able to lend you a pressure gauge and help you plan the circuits.

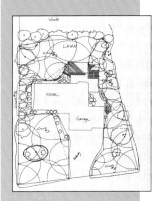

Sprinkler circuits can be drawn on the master plan in their own color, or they can be detailed on a copy of the master plan.

Because underground sprinkler systems tie into the house water supply system, a back-flow prevention valve is usually required – as is a building permit.

Multi-Year Plan

During the planning process you'll start to realize how much all this landscaping could cost, which might be scary. Don't panic – it's not possible to do everything at once, anyway. The key is to break your total scheme into manageable steps. Professionals generally think in terms of three years or five years. This approach allows you to figure out what should be done first and what can wait, and allows you to budget how much time and money to spend each year.

As you organize your five-year plan into more manageable one-year plans, try to complete each area before moving on to the next. If you don't, you're liable to have every part of your yard perpetually torn up and partially completed.

Most people know what they want to do first – what's most important to them. As you think through each project, make a list of the tasks and materials, as well as their sequence. This allows you to get materials delivered as you need them. It also allows you to make a budget and to forecast your cash flow.

Multi-year planning has the added advantage of allowing you to assess each year's results as you make plans for the coming year. It allows you to postpone expense when that's necessary, and to change your mind as you go along.

Shown below is one version of a five-year plan. Yours will likely look different because it will reflect your budget and goals.

Year 1. *Establish a service area so there's a place to put incoming piles of gravel, paving stone, and other materials. Grade the lot and install the sprinkler system. Plant grass or groundcovers. Plant trees and some shrubs.*

Year 2. *Build a deck and make a path to the downstairs patio. Soften the lines of the house with foundation plantings.*

Year 3. Build a retaining wall alongside the house, creating new beds for perennials and shrubs. Hide the air conditioner with shrubs, and establish the vegetable garden.

Year 4. With the major construction out of the way, it's time to make more beds for flowers and vegetables. Careful layout makes the transition from cultivated gardens to woods.

Year 5. A vine-covered arbor and outdoor lighting complete the landscape. Perhaps it's time to enlarge that patio outside the sliding glass doors, and there's probably enough room for a pool…

How big is it?

When you detail your landscape plans, it helps to know how wide a path or a driveway has to be in order to do its job. Of course you can depart from standard sizes any time you've got a good reason for doing so.

Minimum driveway:
9 feet wide
Comfortable driveway: 14 feet wide
Single parking space:
9 feet by 18 feet
Minimum footpath:
24 inches wide
Comfortable pathway:
4 feet wide (This is minimum for wheelchair access.)
Pathway for garden tractors: 6 feet wide
Minimum gateway:
4 feet wide
Privacy fence:
6 feet high
Comfortable ramp for carts or wheelchairs:
4 feet wide, 5 feet of rise per 100 feet of run (5% grade)
Steepest ramp: 12 feet in 100 feet (12% grade)
Narrowest planting bed: 1 foot wide
Border flower bed:
4 feet to 6 feet wide
Vegetable garden:
100 square feet minimum
Small garden shed:
4 feet by 8 feet
Narrowest useful porch or deck:
5 feet

You load 16 tons ...

There's no avoiding it – dirt, gravel, and paving materials are heavy. A cubic yard of gravel weighs about a ton.

A short-handled shovel is best for moving heavy materials. The short handle helps keep the load balanced, while the D grip gives you the control you need. Push with your legs and lower body to load the shovel, pivot or carry it to where it's going, then rotate the grip so the load slides off. Throwing gravel off the shovel just wastes energy; let gravity do it for you.

Who Does What?

Most people are optimistic by nature, so many jobs end up taking twice as long as imagined. Landscaping is fun but it is also a lot of work, and much of that is physically demanding. How much you do yourself depends on your skills and abilities, your finances, and your free time. If you're handy and reasonably fit, it's possible for you to handle any landscaping task yourself. What's important is being realistic. You need whole days, not hurried hours, and it really helps to have assistance. Two people working together can get a lot more done than one person working twice as long.

A professional with the right advice can save you from making expensive mistakes. A professional with the right equipment can save you from a lot of back-breaking or time-consuming labor. Whenever you bring in professional help, be as specific and precise as you can about what you want done, and what you intend to do yourself.

Landscape architects

Landscape architects are trained and licensed professionals who can solve design problems for commercial installations as well as for residences. They can tackle all aspects of the design job, including engineering, and will also supervise construction. If you have a large piece of property and complex plans, a consultation probably will pay off.

Landscape designers

Landscape designers generally limit themselves to residences. Even if they have a great deal of skill and experience, a landscape designer doesn't necessarily have a relevant degree or a state license. Nevertheless, you can expect a designer to solve drainage and grading problems, and to lay out driveways, retaining walls, and terraces. Like architects, landscape designers will not only prepare a plan, but will also supervise construction, if you wish.

Landscape contractors

These are the can-do folks who come in with truck, backhoe, shovel, and wheelbarrow to do the actual construction work. They will create lawns, build walls, and install patios and walkways. Most contractors will discuss your design with you and some may offer design services as well. Landscape contractors are licensed in most (but not all) states.

Nurseries

Nurseries and greenhouses sell plants, and in order to help you choose which ones to buy, some nurseries may also offer design services. Most nurseries will provide referrals for local contractors, leaving you to do the hiring.

Specialty contractors

The Yellow Pages and the bulletin boards at home centers and nurseries can help you find specialty contractors with expertise in such areas as pool design and installation, septic tanks, grading and drainage, and paving.

Hiring a contractor

When you're ready to hire some help, follow up referrals you get from friends, get more than one bid, and check references. Be sure to agree in writing on what work will be done, on what schedule, and what it will cost. Expect to pay some of the money up front, especially if your contractor has to buy materials. Be sure to set a payment schedule with tangible benchmarks. Three payments of 30% is typical, with 10% held back until 45 days after the job is completed. This pro-

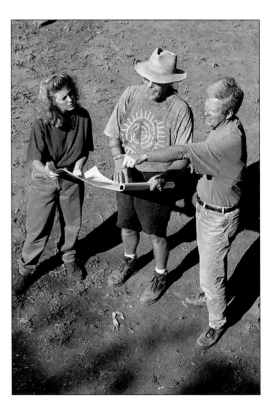

A landscape architect can help you clarify your ideas and unify a variety of projects. The first step is an on-site consultation. Have your plot plan and wish list ready.

Whether you do the work yourself or hire it out, you have to keep control of the plans, details, and budget. Lists, catalogs, clippings, and sketchbooks will all help.

tects you against shoddy work. You also need a lien waiver from the contractor, which protects you against claims for payment by suppliers or subcontractors. You also should have insurance protection against the risk that someone gets hurt while working on your property, so check with the agent for your homeowner's policy. Your contractor should carry his own liability and workers compensation insurance.

Permits and inspections

Landscape work has to conform to zoning regulations, but it generally does not require the maze of permits that residential construction does. Nevertheless, each state and locality will have its own regulations and it's up to the homeowner to find out what applies. Most towns have regulations governing fence heights and setbacks from the property line. Structures such as decks usually require a permit, as do 110-volt electrical work and most new plumbing. If you're landscaping near a running stream or a bog, you may need permission from your local wetlands conservation agency as well.

To find out what permits are necessary, ask the building department at your town hall or municipal center. Usually you will have to submit a drawing of your proposed work. When you receive a permit, post it where it can be seen and, if it calls for inspections, make sure you arrange to have them done.

Condominium developments and some subdivisions may have their own regulations covering what homeowners may add to their property. It's also possible that your deed includes an easement of some sort, for a utility company, for a future sidewalk or road widening, or for a neighbor's right-of-way. The specific language of the easement will tell you what you can and can't do with that part of your yard. It's up to you to check the deed and make any necessary inquiries.

Get building permits as required by local codes, and post the permits where they can be seen.

Work-site safety

A clean work site is the key to safety. Clear away construction debris at the end of every work day. Don't leave tools where people can step on them.

To protect yourself while working, wear suitable clothing. Wear long pants, gloves, and work boots and, if you're working under the hot sun, a hat. Wear eye protection when you're hammering and around power saws and other chip-making machinery, and wear ear protection around noisy machinery.

Use tools only for their intended purpose, and store them safely when you're done. Put sharp tools (like loppers and saws) away where kids can't get at them. Stash your rake with the tines down or toward the wall.

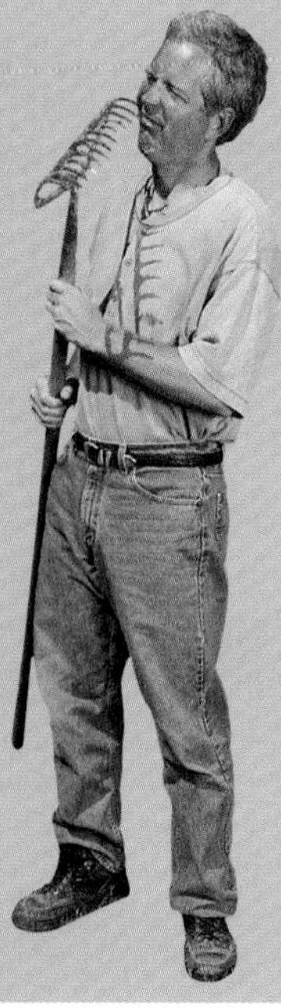

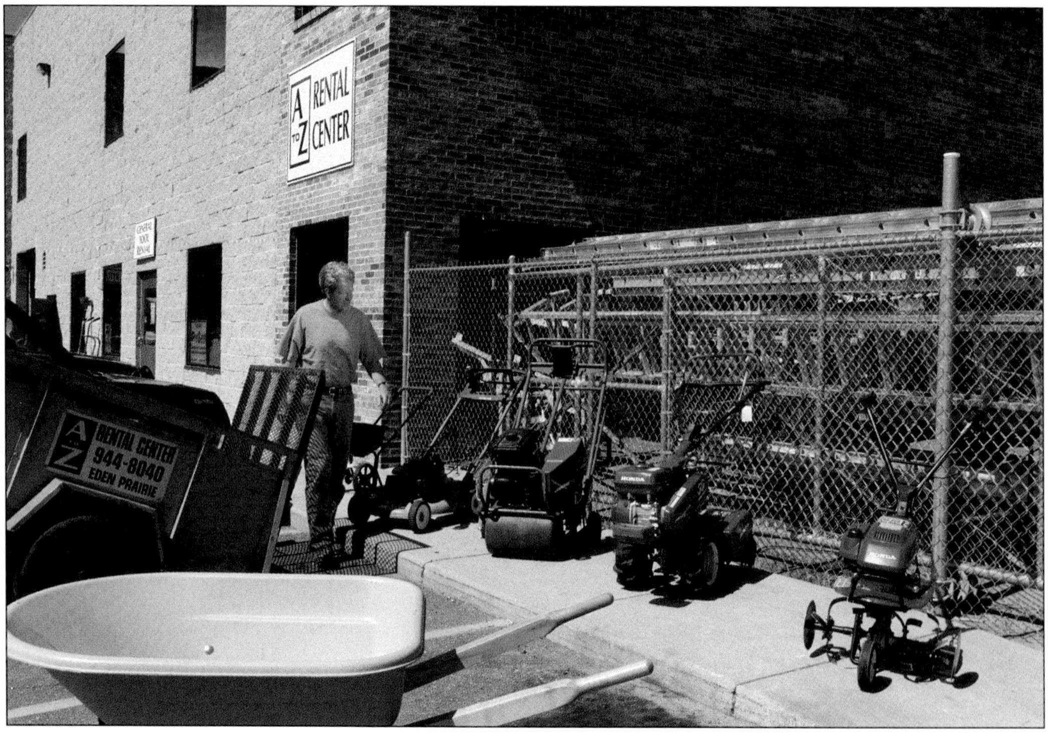

You can rent almost anything, *so you don't have to own every tool in the world. Buy tools you'll need to use over and over again, like shovels and wheelbarrows. Rent tools you need for a day or two, like transits and concrete mixers.*

Buy Good Tools

Having the right tools can make difficult jobs seem easy. The sensible strategy is to buy the tools you'll use over and over again. Buy the best basic tools you can afford, and take care of them so they last. Add specialty tools as they come up, but consider renting them instead. If it's big and expensive, like a power washer or a concrete mixer, you'll probably be able to rent a bigger and tougher model than you could afford to buy, anyway.

Here are some basic tools every homeowner should own.

For measuring: 25-foot and 100-foot tape measures, framing square, carpenter's speed square, 4-foot level, plumb bob, mason's line with line level.

Hand tools: framing hammer, sledge hammer, short toolbox saw with coarse teeth, chisel, heavy wirecutter, hacksaw, Surform rasp, several sizes of pliers and screwdrivers, awl, putty knife, pocket knife.

Power tools: cordless drill, jig saw, circular saw, 50-foot outdoor extension cord.

For handling and hauling: wheelbarrow, garden cart, pair of sawhorses, extension ladder long enough to reach your roof from the ground.

For digging: long-handled spade, short-handled square-nose mason's shovel, 4-foot pry bar, pick, mattock, rake.

For concrete and masonry: mortar trowel, margin trowel, pointing trowel, concrete float.

For yard maintenance: lawn mower, lawn edger, pruning shears, hedge clipper, leaf rake.

For safety: work boots with steel toes, goggles with side shields, hearing protectors, dust mask, gloves.

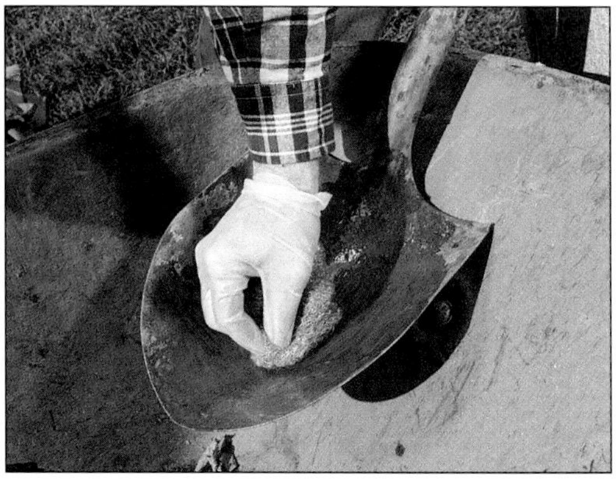

Good tools will last *as long as you do, provided you clean them and keep them in good shape. Steel wool and naval jelly remove rust and stubborn crud.*

GRADING and DRAINAGE

The slope of your land determines how the water flows, *so if the land slopes toward the house, that's where the water will flow, and that's the first grading problem to solve. Flowing water also causes erosion, so if you're watching your topsoil wash away in the rain, you've got another grading issue to resolve. Moving earth to change the grade and digging trenches to lay drains generally make a mess of whatever's in the way. That's why taking care of grading and drainage is the first order of business – before you tackle any other landscaping projects.*

Making the Grade

Begin your drainage survey by taking a hard look at what happens during heavy rain. If water comes into the basement, mark exactly where it enters, then wade outside to find the source. Assess the gutters and downspouts, and find where they empty. Does the water flow away, or does it puddle against the foundation?

Measuring grades and elevations

Landscapers specify slopes by indicating the drop over a given distance. A slope of 1 inch in 4 feet (a 2% grade) is the minimum for water to flow across a hard-surfaced driveway, sidewalk, or patio. Over short distances, you can measure grade with a tape measure and a long carpenter's level. Over longer distances, use a line level, water level, surveyor's transit, builder's level, or laser level.

Dig we must

The simplest and most direct way to move earth is with pick, shovel, and wheelbarrow. Slice off any usable turf. Store the sod in shade, either rolled or laid flat; it will keep for about a week if you don't let it dry out. Separate the topsoil into its own pile, so you can use it again. Break up the subsoil and grub out the boulders and roots.

Measure grade over short distances with a straight 2x4 and a level. Raise the low end until the bubble indicates level, then measure the drop. For convenience, tape the level to the 2x4.

If the area you're grading is too large to tackle with shovel and rake, you can always call in a landscaping contractor. A skilled operator with a small skid loader can rearrange a large chunk of landscape in no time at all.

Laser level 101

You can rent a laser level to measure elevations. It shoots a beam of red laser light from a rotating turret. You take the measurement by watching where the laser light strikes the height rod. It can be difficult to see the light beam in daylight, but most laser levels come with an electronic pickup that emits a beep when the light strikes it. An advantage of the laser level over a transit or a builder's level is that one person can work it alone.

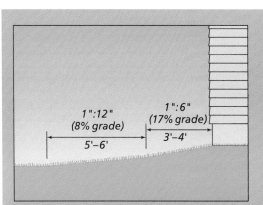

1":12" (8% grade) 5'-6'
1":6" (17% grade) 3'-4'

The grade must slope away from the foundation of the house on all sides. It should drop 1 inch in every 6 inches near the foundation, and 1 inch in 12 inches for the next 5 to 6 feet.

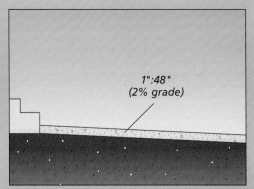

1":48" (2% grade)

Paths and walkways should slope about 2% away from the building. This holds true whether the path leads up to the house or runs alongside it.

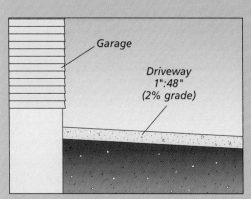

Garage
Driveway *1":48"* (2% grade)

Driveways and other hard surfaces need a 2% slope, or 1 inch in 48 inches. When the existing grade can only run downhill toward the garage, install a drain the width of the pavement right outside the garage doors.

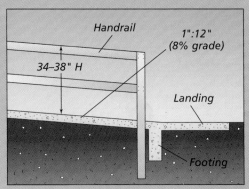

Handrail
1":12" (8% grade)
34–38" H
Landing
Footing

A wheelchair access ramp should slope no more than 8%, or 1 inch in 12 inches; it's difficult to propel a chair up a steeper slope. The ramp also needs a 5-foot-square landing at top and bottom for easy maneuvering.

Protecting trees

Tree roots spread at least as far underground as their branches spread above; the imaginary circle described by the branches is called the drip zone. You can't do much inside the drip zone without harming or killing the tree. If you bang equipment into the bark, you'll damage it. If you dig near the trunk, you'll cut some roots. If you add soil inside the drip zone, or drive heavy equipment over it, you may smother the roots. And if you pave over the drip zone, you can starve the tree of both water and oxygen. During major projects we usually stake bright orange mesh around the drip zone to keep heavy equipment away.

Even the smallest machine will leave a mess, but cleaning up is still less work than moving the dirt yourself.

Divide grading into two stages, rough and finish. Work out a logical sequence, so you don't get in your own way. Complete all the rough grading, then install drains and any other underground utilities before filling holes and raking the surface smooth.

Large projects *may require power equipment like this skid loader. While you can rent one, you're probably better off hiring a contractor. The machine can move earth, dig trenches, and shift piles of materials.*

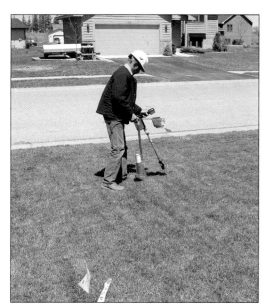

Before you dig, *make sure that buried utility lines and pipes are located and marked. In most areas, there's a free one-call utility locating service that will send someone out to find and mark the lines on your property.*

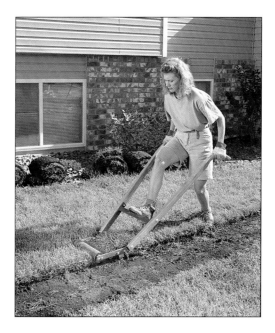

Remove grass *with a sharp spade or a sod cutter (manual and gas-powered versions are available at rental centers). This is the easiest method, whether you plan to reuse the turf or not.*

Solving Drainage Problems

When you are dealing with large amounts of runoff, or with subsurface water, a simple grade change may not be enough. You may need to install drains, catch basins, or drywells.

Before you start to dig, plan each drain line. Start from where you want the water to go (called the outfall), and work back to the source. Drain each area to a central point, then drain that to the outfall. The pipe should drop at least ⅛ inch per foot, and it must dump the water into a storm sewer, catch basin, or out to daylight where it can flow harmlessly away. Drain the water from your property into the community's gutters and storm sewers, not into the sanitary sewers or into your own septic system. It's never polite to dump your runoff water onto your neighbor's property, and in many areas it is illegal.

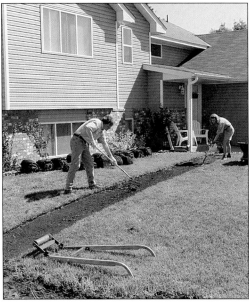

Dig a swale, or shallow ditch, to carry runoff away from the house. Grade the earth so the water flows down into the swale from either side.

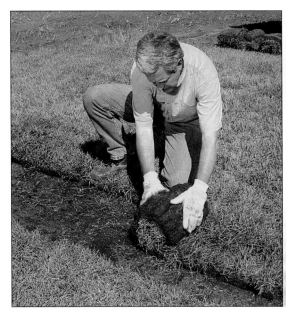

Shape the swale, tamp the earth, then re-lay the sod. This simple solution will direct a surprising amount of water away from the house.

Drainage problem checklist

- Water on the basement floor. This is a major problem to solve right away, so find out where it's coming from. The solution may be as simple as grading, or as expensive as installing a drain. A curtain drain outside the foundation requires digging right down to the base of the wall. A perimeter drain inside the house requires cutting a trench in the concrete floor.

- Water condensing on the basement floors and walls. Install dehumidifiers, air-condition the space, or add insulation to the outside of the walls.

- Water seeping through the basement walls. Regrading outside the wall may control it, but if not, you may need to install a drain. Unfortunately, masonry paints probably won't help.

- Puddles against the foundation of the house. Regrade so the water flows away.

- Eroded gullies washing soil away. Control the source of the water. Break up the flow so the water has time to soak into the ground.

- Soggy lawn. Lower the water table with a perforated drain pipe and catch basins.

Drainage solutions at a glance

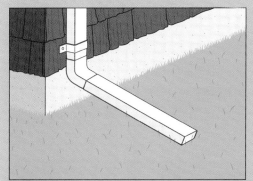

Downspout extension

Water from the downspouts has to flow away from the house. Sometimes all that's needed is a simple extension to carry it 2 to 4 feet away. If that doesn't help, connect the downspout to an underground drain line, either directly or through a catch basin.

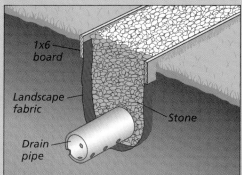

French drain

A French drain can catch and move a lot of surface runoff along with subsurface water. Dig the drainage ditch and make sure it slopes at least 2 inches in 10 feet. Line the ditch with landscape fabric and lay the perforated drain pipe in a bed of gravel or crushed rock. The holes should face downward so subsurface water can rise into the pipe. Cover the pipe and fill the ditch with gravel. The gravel channels runoff to the drain and protects the pipe from being crushed.

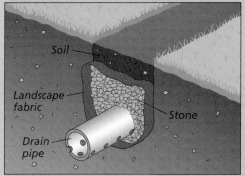

Buried drain pipe

If a buried drain doesn't have to pick up surface water along part of its route, the trench can be lined with landscape fabric or soil filter cloth (a kind of landscape fabric that helps protects the drain system from silting up), and hidden under a layer of sod. If the pipe has holes only on one side, lay it with the holes face down so water will rise into the pipe; otherwise, the holes clog with silt and debris.

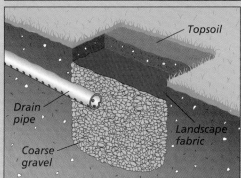

Dry well

A dry well is a deep hole filled with gravel where a swale or an underground drain can empty. There's a limit to how much water can be dumped into a dry well, but it depends completely on local conditions and building regulations. A dry well usually needs a cap, which can be a concrete pad or landscape fabric buried under a layer of gravel or topsoil and topped with sod.

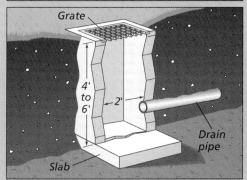

Catch basin

A catch basin can help drain a low spot, and it's also a way to dump surface water into an underground drainage system. You can pour a concrete catch basin, but in many situations a simple plastic one is all you'll need. The grate lifts up so you can clean accumulated sediment out of the basin.

Controlling Erosion

Along with poor drainage comes erosion. When water runs too quickly over the land, it can wash away the topsoil, creating gullies and ditches. To control erosion you need to divert and slow the flow of water.

Plantings

A thick planting may be all you need to cover a problem hillside, slow down surface runoff, and retain the soil. The leaves and stems deflect the incoming water, while the roots hold the soil in a tight mass. Choosing plants and low shrubs with a suitable root structure depends on your climate zone, so consult a local nursery.

Erosion control blankets

A layer of erosion control fabric can help hold the topsoil on a medium slope. The material has to be porous, such as burlap or plastic mesh made for landscaping. Smooth the fabric over the ground and cut holes in it to plant ground cover. The fabric eventually rots, but not before the plants' roots trap the topsoil.

Riprap

A problem hillside or shoreline can be covered with concrete rubble or boulders, called riprap. The riprap breaks up the flow of water and helps lock the soil in place. Bury boulders about half-way, packing soil tightly around each one. Plant a ground cover between boulders to hold the soil in place.

Retaining walls

Serious erosion can be controlled with retaining walls, which can transform almost any slope into a series of level planting beds. Bury perforated drain lines behind the walls to carry the water away.

Plants help control erosion two ways. Roots help hold the soil in place, while the plant stems break up and slow the flow of surface water.

Riprap holds the soil in place on steep slopes. Along shorelines, it slows the flow of water from above and serves as a breakwater to keep waves from eroding the shore.

Erosion control blankets hold the soil on a medium slope until plants can establish a network of roots. The biodegradable plastic mesh is interwoven with shredded poplar.

Retaining walls break steep slopes with serious erosion problems into manageable terraces. This breaks the flow of water and creates level planting areas.

RETAINING WALLS

Retaining walls can make interesting and useful spaces *out of land-scape problems. Walls hold back the earth, transforming slopes into level terraces or creating raised beds for planting. You can build a small wall to isolate a tree from the surrounding lawn and to create a flower bed around it. A larger wall or a series of walls will transform a hard-to-mow slope into level terraces for flowers and shrubs. Single walls up to three feet or four feet high usually can be designed and built by homeowners. Higher walls may require professional design and construction assistance.*

Planning the Wall

The first step in planning your retaining wall is to stake its ends and lay out its shape with an old garden hose. Later, when you're ready to start work, you can mark the shape by sprinkling lime or spraying paint along the hose. Make a bird's eye drawing of the proposed site and sketch the wall, then draw the cross-section of the wall at its highest point. You'll need all this information to figure out how much material to order.

Instead of making a single high wall with a large terrace at the top, break slopes into several small terraces supported by a series of low walls. That way you'll avoid engineering complications, and you'll be able to do the work in stages, starting from the bottom and working up. You'll also have a lot less earth to excavate.

Even a low terrace bears a great deal of weight, especially when the soil is wet. The steeper the slope, the higher the wall, the heavier the load bearing on the wall. Parking cars or putting buildings atop a wall increases the load, too. This is why you should seek professional advice when planning a wall higher than 4 feet. In most places you'll have to get a building permit for any wall higher than 3 feet or 4 feet, which means one or more inspections as the work progresses. Local regulations vary, so be sure to check.

Materials

Although raised beds and garden walls are often made of treated wooden timbers, they're not necessarily the best choice. Timber walls need more maintenance than masonry ones, and even the best installation ultimately will rot.

Another popular choice for do-it-yourselfers is to build walls with interlocking concrete block. Some styles interlock by means of flanges cast into the back edge, while others have vertical holes for fiberglass locking pins. They come in various surface finishes and colors and, depending on the size, weigh in at anywhere from 15 to 75 pounds per block.

The 2:1 rule

When you divide a slope into terraces, you have to set the

upper wall back from the lower one to reduce the load on the lower wall. Use the 2-to-1 rule to determine the setback from one wall to the next. For every foot of height in the lower wall, there should be two feet of terrace leading to the next wall. For example, if the lower wall is 4 feet high, the terrace that it supports should be at least 8 feet wide. You can sometimes reduce the amount of setback by using geogrid to stabilize the soil (see page 28).

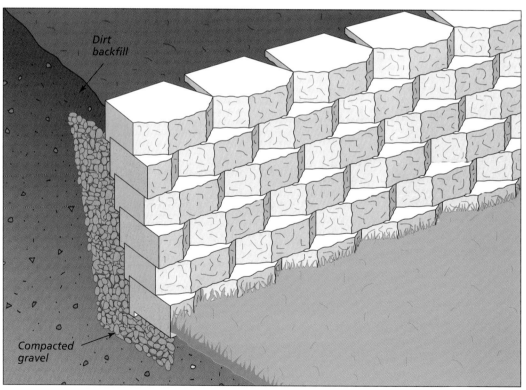

Dirt backfill

Compacted gravel

Anatomy of a retaining wall. *The foundation for a retaining wall is a 3- to 6-inch layer of compacted gravel or coarse sand. Each course is also backfilled with the base material. Dry-laid walls are held in place by gravity. Setting each course back from the previous one helps gravity do its job. Here, flanges on the back of the blocks provide the right amount of setback from course to course. Other block systems use pins to lock each course in place.*

Stone, while typically more expensive than concrete block or landscape timbers, is also frequently chosen for wall construction. You can build a stone wall using uncut field-stone, but it's much easier to work with flat slabs, such as sandstone or dolomite. These stones may vary a lot in thickness and size, but since the broad surfaces are flat, the wall is not difficult to piece together.

Wet and dry

There are two basic types of masonry wall, dry and wet. A dry wall means the stones or blocks fit together without the addition of mortar, though sometimes one course has to be glued to the next with masonry adhesive. A dry wall is often called a gravity wall or a dry-laid wall. Water can escape from behind the wall through the spaces between the blocks.

A wet wall has mortar joints between the stones or blocks. The mortar locks the individual blocks or stones into a solid mass. It also prevents water from seeping through the wall, making a drainage system necessary.

Wall foundations

A low wall under 3 feet can be bedded directly on stable soil, but if there's any doubt about stability, lay a bed of compacted gravel a few inches thick. Walls 3 feet and higher, and walls built on unstable soil or steep slopes, should be bedded on 6 inches of compacted fill, such as coarse sand or class 5 (¾-inch minus) crushed stone. As a rule of thumb, there should be about an inch of wall below grade for every 8 inches above grade. This means the bottom course of block will be mostly, or even completely, underground.

Drainage

Dry-laid walls, if they're low and not in the path of torrential run-off, generally have enough gaps to drain by themselves. You can improve drainage by leaving ½-inch spaces between the blocks in the bottom two rows. Mortared walls will need drain pipe buried in gravel behind the base of the wall. If you're not sure whether to install drain pipe, go ahead and do it. Otherwise the wall is liable to fail prematurely due to the pressure of trapped water, which is made worse in cold climates by freeze-thaw cycles.

Choosing materials

The wall-building materials shown below are typical of the wide variety available at home centers and through specialized masonry suppliers.

Use your site drawing to calculate the square footage of the face of your wall by multiplying the length times the height – don't forget to include the below-grade part of the wall. To figure curves, calculate the outside face of the curve, just as if it were stretched out flat. Be sure to add 10% to the total to account for cuts and waste.

Interlocking concrete blocks come in various surface finishes and colors and are in the middle of the price range for wall materials. Many have tapered sides, allowing them to follow a curving layout.

Mortared block is reinforced with metal stakes driven into the ground through the block cavities. Block looks industrial, but can be faced with stucco or a decorative veneer of brick or stone.

Cut stone comes in many varieties and colors. It can be laid dry or with mortar. High walls must be laid two stones deep (one behind the other) and connected with tie stones. Cut stone is at the high end of the price scale.

Fieldstone walls are made of dry-laid uncut stone, or rubble, fit together like a three-dimensional jigsaw puzzle. Fieldstone isn't expensive if you choose a local variety, not one that has been shipped in.

Pressure-treated wooden timbers last for a long time, but will eventually rot and have to be replaced. Timber is about the same price as interlocking block.

Building bricks, shown here mortared into a running bond pattern, have to be laid two deep, connected by tie bricks laid crosswise at regular intervals. Brick is relatively expensive.

Cast concrete retaining walls are relatively inexpensive, but labor intensive to build. The concrete can be colored, making it a good option when you just can't find stone or block of the right color or size.

Interlocking Block Walls

Although there are a lot of wall-building materials to choose from, interlocking concrete blocks are designed with features that simplify the work for homeowners. They're laid dry, and they have tapered sides so the same block can be used to build straight or curved wall sections. This means you don't have to do much cutting.

With a dry-laid wall, what holds the wall up is its own weight. This means the setback from one course to the next is critical; without the setback it's possible for the weight of the backfill to shove the blocks forward. The blocks have flanges or pins that guarantee the right amount of setback.

Interlocking concrete blocks are easy to work with and the work goes relatively fast. The general sequence of steps doesn't change, but some of the details depend on the specific brand of blocks you buy, so read and follow the manufacturer's instructions. Choosing the best materials for the base and for backfill may also depend on local soil conditions and building practices, so ask the block dealer for recommendations.

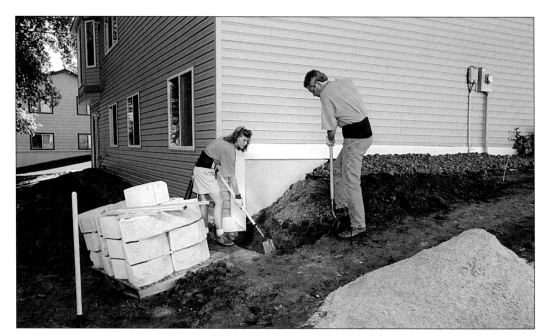

1 **Dig a trench** 14 inches wide along the path of the wall. It should be about a foot deep to accommodate a six-inch gravel base plus the buried course of block that acts as the wall's foundation. Skim the bottom of the trench flat and smooth without disturbing the underlying soil.

2 **Pack a 6-inch base layer** of coarse sand or compactible fill into the trench. Pack the base down hard with a tamper or a length of 4x4 timber.

3 **Make the base material** as level as possible. The base will affect the whole wall you build on it, so take the time to get it right. Stake a mason's line along the back side of the wall to help keep the base course straight.

4 *Set the first course* of block on the base. If the base is sand, you can dig a groove to fit the flange on the back bottom edge of the blocks. If the base is gravel, you'll have to chip the flanges off the blocks so they'll sit flat.

5 *Level and align* the blocks starting at the lowest point. If a block is low, add coarse sand underneath it. If it's high, tap it into the base material with a rubber mallet. A little extra space between blocks will help the wall drain.

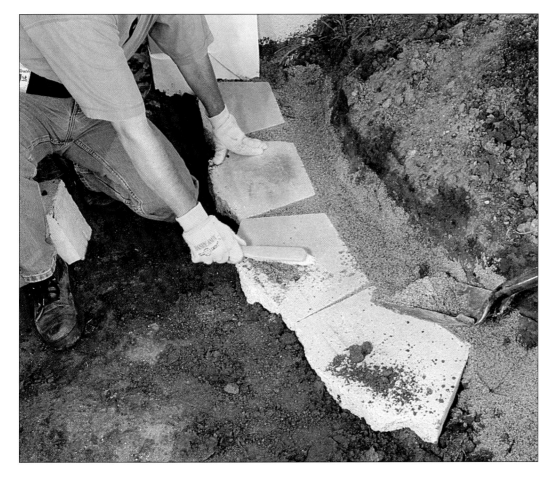

6 *Backfill* the foundation course of blocks with coarse sand or the same aggregate used for the base. To keep them from shifting, fill in all around the blocks. Tamp the backfill with a chunk of 4x4. Sweep off the top surface of the blocks before setting the next course.

Reinforcing the soil

Geogrid is the general name for a family of materials that can be used to stabilize slopes and to tie multiple retaining walls together. This material is a tough, dense, and long-lasting mesh made of high-density polyethylene or woven polyester fibers. The open mesh allows water to percolate freely through the fabric so it doesn't interfere with drainage.

Geogrid usually is installed as a horizontal layer buried in the fill behind a retaining wall, with at least 8 inches of the front edge of the geogrid trapped between two courses of block. The soil beneath the grid has to be compacted and raked smooth. Then the fabric must be spread and staked flat. More fill goes on top of the geogrid, locking it in place.

In some terracing situations, the back edge of the geogrid should be trapped between courses of block in the next wall up the slope. High walls and terraces that must support heavy loads may need more than one horizontal layer of geogrid, separated by 18 inches to 2 feet of fill. Properly installed, geogrid will tie a series of walls into a single system, helping

to distribute the load and to transfer it down to the earth at the base. Tying an upper wall to the one below can also allow you to break the 2-to-1 setback rule, but you should get professional advice before you try this.

Setting the blocks

In a dry-laid wall, it's important to make sure each course of block sits square and level on the one below. The flange at the back of the block hooks over the block beneath. This means that each course of block steps back as the wall goes up. This setback, or batter, helps the wall resist the load of soil and water behind it.

When the wall dies into a slope, you will end up placing a full block over a half block in the course below. In that situation, be sure to prepare a firm bed of base material underneath the overhanging block, just as you did for the foundation row.

1 ***Carefully level each block*** *as you go. Make sure it is level from side to side and from front to back, and that it ends up at exactly the same height as the blocks on either side.*

2 ***Make sure the flange*** *hooks over the block below. Set each block, then pull it forward so the flange contacts the back of the block below. This ensures the setback is correct from one course to the next.*

3 ***If the backfill*** *is dirt or coarse sand, lay a barrier of permeable landscape fabric behind the bottom few courses of block to keep the backfill from washing through the blocks.*

Large walls and steep slopes need more drainage than the spaces between blocks can provide. Excess water will eat away at the backfill, eroding the wall's foundations, and on large walls, hydrostatic pressure will shove the blocks out of place. To avoid water problems, install perforated drain pipe to collect the water and carry it away from the backfill. Lay a barrier of permeable landscape fabric in the bottom of the trench behind the wall and lap it up a couple of courses. Shovel in a layer of clean-draining aggregate, then run perforated drain pipe along the wall and out to daylight, either at the end of the wall or through a space between the blocks. Bury the pipe in the backfill as you add courses to the wall.

4 **Tamp the backfill** behind each course. Sweep the blocks clean, then place and level the next row. Note that as the wall dies into the slope, the end block of each course rests partly on the block below and partly on a compacted base.

Cutting and splitting concrete block

You'll need to trim blocks to compensate for the setback as the wall rises, to make corners, and to make the blocks fit neatly against adjacent walls or foundations. There are two ways to do this, splitting and cutting. Splitting a block creates a rough-textured face, while cutting leaves a smooth face. Always wear safety goggles as protection against flying chips of concrete.

Hammer and chisel. Score the block on each side, then split it by pounding the chisel into the score line. Hammer off any stray protrusions. If your wall has split-face blocks, always split corner units so there will be a rough finish on both exposed faces.

Block splitter. If you have a lot of blocks to split, rent a hydraulic block splitter to break the block on the layout line.

Masonry saw. For a clean, smooth cut, rent a large cut-off saw. If the block is deeper than the saw's capacity, square the layout line onto the other faces and cut each side.

Score the block along the lines, using a circular saw with a diamond-tipped blade or a Carborundum blade. Make the cuts an inch deep.

Split the block by driving a cold chisel into the scored line. This makes a rough face, matching the one on the front of the block.

Corners and curves

Step blocks are often used for corners because they have squared sides, instead of tapered. They have a rough texture only on the front face, so you'll have to split the blocks to get a rough texture on both faces of the corner. To build a strong corner, make sure to interweave the corner blocks: if the corner block in one course extends to the right, the one in the next row should extend to the left. The blocks used to turn corners don't have flanges, so use masonry adhesive to hold them in place.

Rounding curves with tapered blocks is easy. Since the sides are tapered, you won't have to cut the blocks. On tight curves, however, you might have to break off the outer edges of the flanges to allow the block to slide far enough forward.

bring the pattern back in phase.

On curved walls the joint pattern is less conspicuous, so let the joints drift until one joint lines up directly over another. At that point, cut a block to bridge the joint and get the pattern back on track.

Building steps

If you need frequent access to the terrace behind a wall, incorporate steps into the wall design. Special step blocks have straight, not tapered, sides. They are usually the same height as the wall units, so you can weave the steps into the wall.

Lay each step course when you lay the wall course it fits into. Bed each tread on compacted fill, as if it were the foundation course of a new wall. Use masonry adhesive to lock the blocks in place.

Split corner blocks to make a decorative face on both visible surfaces. Strengthen the corners by interweaving the blocks. The cut blocks next to the corner blocks help maintain the running bond pattern.

Step blocks have square sides that fit tightly together. When setting the blocks, make sure each tread is the same depth. Step blocks don't have flanges; bond them with masonry adhesive.

Joint spacing

Each course you add to a wall with corners or curves is shorter than the row below it (think of pyramids and igloos). As the rows get shorter this will affect the alignment of the joints from row to row. To keep one joint from lining up over another joint (what the pros call walking off bond), you'll have to trim one or more blocks to bring everything back in line.

With walls that have corners, build the straight sections for each course first, then cut and fit the blocks for the corner. Sometimes you can maintain the running bond pattern by planning carefully where you will split the corner block. Other times you'll also have to cut the block next to the corner to

Cap blocks

Some walls don't require any special topping off. If their terraces will be planted with low evergreens, you'll probably never see the top of the wall. But when the wall runs alongside a walkway or borders a flower garden, you might want a more finished look. Many styles of block include caps, though you may have to special-order them.

It's up to you whether the caps sit flush with the front face of the wall, overhang it, or sit back a bit. It's simply a matter of what looks best to you. If the wall is straight, string a mason's line to guide you. If the wall is curved or stepped, cut a wooden block the depth of the setback or overhang, and use it as a gauge.

Lay out the cap blocks using a mason's string to get the cap blocks straight. Trace a line along the back of the blocks onto the blocks below, and then remove a few of the blocks.

Since cap blocks are thinner and lighter than regular block, they should be glued in place with a few dabs of masonry adhesive. Place the caps, trace their layout onto the blocks below, and then remove them. Sweep the surface clean, apply the adhesive, then replace the caps, aligning them to the marks you made. This technique avoids gluing any caps in the wrong place.

Sweep the surface clean, apply some masonry adhesive, then replace the caps, aligning them to the line you made. Do a couple caps at a time to avoid gluing any caps in the wrong place.

Fiberglass pins connect the blocks

Working with pinned blocks isn't all that different from building with flanged blocks. Before you backfill behind each new course, just drop the fiberglass pins into the holes in the blocks. This way, the backfill won't plug up the holes and interfere with the pins. Backfill, then sweep off the blocks, add a few dabs of concrete adhesive, and set the next block over the pins.

Fiberglass pins drop into holes cast into the blocks. The pins locate and lock the next course in place.

Apply several blobs of masonry adhesive near the pins so the blocks can't shift around.

Set each block over the pins in the course below. To maintain the right setback, nudge each block as far forward as the pins will allow it to go.

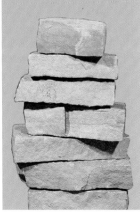

Dry-Laid Stone Walls

Stone walls should be built two stones deep (each layer is called a leaf.) Bed the wall on a 6-inch compacted layer of crushed gravel, and bury most of the first course, which should be made with the largest stones you have. Stagger the joints in each leaf so they don't line up. Use tie stones, or bonding stones, to connect the two leaves; add them at intervals to every third or fourth course. Long stones called deadmen extend through the wall into the fill behind. Deadmen and tie stones should not be next to one another, but they can be in the same course.

As with any dry-laid wall, each course of stone should be set back about a half-inch from the course below. Cap the wall with tie stones, which can be laid dry or mortared.

Dry-laid stone walls look informal and natural. The color of the stone works with the rest of the landscape. The more variation in the size of the stones, the more irregular the finished wall.

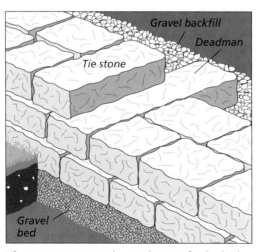

Tie stones connect the two leaves of a dry-laid stone wall. Longer stones called deadmen tie the wall into the slope.

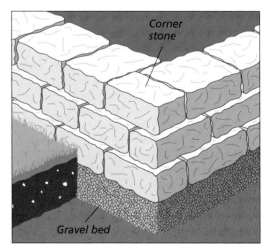

Interlock the stones at the corners, and cap the wall with broad tie stones spanning both leaves.

Timber Walls

Landscape timbers are easy to work with because they can be cut and drilled with ordinary woodworking tools. On the other hand, since timber isn't as heavy as stone or concrete, a timber wall needs more engineer-ing. It has to be tied into the backfill with a system of deadmen and sleepers, and it must have good drainage at the base.

Pressure treatment helps the timbers resist bacterial attack. However, you don't want to get the stuff in your system, so wear gloves and a dust mask when sawing.

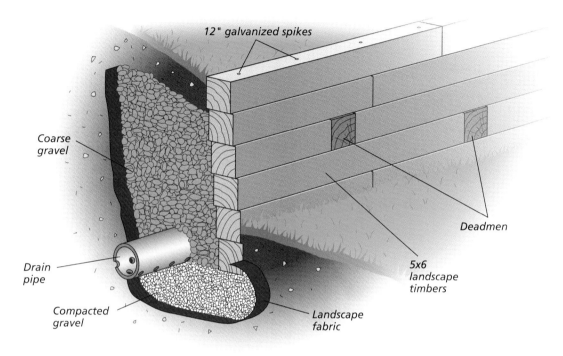

12" galvanized spikes

Coarse gravel

Drain pipe

Compacted gravel

Landscape fabric

5x6 landscape timbers

Deadmen

Compact a 6-inch base of gravel or sand over a layer of landscape fabric. Anchor the foundation timbers with 3-foot lengths of steel reinforcing rod, or rebar, driven through predrilled holes into the earth below. Place a perforated drain pipe about 6 inches behind the foundation timbers, then backfill both with coarse gravel. Set each course back about ½ inch from the one below and tie them together with 12-inch-long galva-nized spikes driven at each end of the timber and every 12 to 18 inches in between.

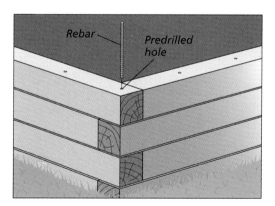

Rebar

Predrilled hole

Make corners by interlocking the timbers log-cabin style. Carefully pre-drill each corner timber with a centered 1-inch hole so you can anchor the entire corner by driving a length of ¾-inch steel rebar down into the soil below.

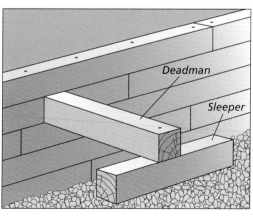

Deadman

Sleeper

Deadmen and sleepers tie the wall into the backfill. Make them about 3 feet long. Tamp the backfill, then set the deadmen in the middle courses of the wall, spaced about 6 feet apart. Spike each deadman into the course below, then bed the sleeper in the backfill and spike it to the free end of the deadman.

Buying timbers

Pressure-treated land-scape timbers gener-ally are sold as 5x6, 6x6 and 6x8 in size, in 8-foot lengths. As with all milled lumber, the nominal dimen-sion is not the actual dimension. A 6x6 measures 5½ inches on a side, while a 6x8 landscape tie actually measures 5½ by 7½. Keep the actual sizes of the timbers in mind when planning your wall.

Raised Beds

A raised bed is just another form of retaining wall. You can make a raised bed with any of the retaining wall materials, including wood. However, if you plan to grow vegetables, you'll have to decide what you think about pressure-treated wood. The manufacturers say it's no problem, but many people worry that the preservative chemicals will leach into the soil and show up in the veggies. The alternative is a naturally rot resistant wood such as redwood, cedar, cypress, or black locust.

Why a raised bed?

Many gardeners believe the best way to keep the soil loose for good plant growth is to dig it deep and then never walk on it again. That's one good reason for building a raised bed. Other reasons include isolating the bed from poor surrounding soil, raising the garden to a convenient working height, protecting the garden from inadvertent trampling, and intensive vegetable gardening.

1 *To square the sides* of the bed, measure 3 feet from the corner along the existing side, and 4 feet from the corner along the layout line. Then swing the line until the two points are exactly 5 feet apart.

2 *Use 36-inch lengths* of 6x6 timber for the posts. Cut and chisel notches 15 inches long and 1½ inches deep to hold the 2x8 sides of the bed.

3 *The posts* have to be plumb and square to the layout lines. Pour a bed of gravel in the hole, then add or subtract gravel to adjust the height of the posts.

4 *The side boards* fit inside the posts so they can resist the weight of the soil. Drop the 2x8s into position and fasten them to the posts with 3-inch galvanized screws.

5 *Fill the bed* with topsoil, add any soil amendments, and let it settle through a couple of rain showers. Then fill it up again before planting.

SOIL PREPARATION

Whether you're starting a new planting bed or maintaining an old one, the condition of the soil is critical. Plants rely on their root systems for good health, and roots rely on the soil to provide the food and water they need. Without good soil, your gardening efforts are bound to be disappointing.

Friable is a word you often hear in connection with good, fertile soil. It means loose and crumbly – easy for moisture to soak in and for a plant's roots to push through as they grow and develop. The path to friable soil isn't complicated, but it can be labor intensive. Is the work worth it? Absolutely. Once your soil is up to par it's easy to keep that way, and you will be rewarded for your efforts with flourishing plants.

Soil Preparation

The right soil gives your plants easy access to nutrients and water. If yours is less than perfect, don't worry; even the poorest soils can be improved.

All soils contain sand, clay, silt, and organic matter called humus. It's the proportion of these materials that make a soil good or poor for gardening. Soil with lots of clay traps water and doesn't drain well, often resulting in root rot. Sandy soils drain so quickly that plants can't absorb the water and nutrients they need. Loam soil, which is what you want, has enough clay to hold water, and enough sand to drain before the roots get soggy.

Soil tests

The first step to soil improvement is soil analysis. You can test your soil with a home kit, or you can send samples to a lab. Most home test kits check for four factors: pH level, nitrogen (abbreviated as N), phosphorous (P), and potassium (K).

Computerized test results from a state agricultural service or a university lab are more accurate and give more information than home kits. You send a soil sample in a plastic bag, and they will tell you how much organic matter is present in your soil, how to adjust the acid balance, or pH, and which elements your soil needs most. Laboratories may charge for this service, which usually takes a couple of weeks.

When gathering samples for a soil test, collect soil from various areas of the planting bed, digging down several inches for each one. Mix all of the samples together.

Improving soil

Improving the soil can be as simple as rototilling to loosen it up and adding compost on a regular basis. You may also add amendments to change its composition, such as fertilizers, nutrients, and bulk organic materials like peat moss. Even if you decide to live with your soil as is, becoming familiar with its properties will help you select the plants that are most likely to thrive.

Making compost

Compost is created when organic matter breaks down. It's great food for your soil, and composting your yard waste helps save landfill space. Good compost is full of earthworms, which help keep soil friable; they also add valuable organic matter as they tunnel beneath the surface.

You can add small pieces of any waste plant material from the vegetable or flower garden, lawn, or kitchen to the compost bin, but avoid meats, bones, and pet wastes. An equal mixture of dried brown material (old leaves and straw) and fresh green material (grass and vegetable scraps) will help prevent foul odors from developing. Compost must be piled 2 feet or 3 feet high, kept moist, and stirred occasionally. This allows heat to build up, hastening decomposition. Compost starters, called innoculants, can help speed up the process, but adding compete fertilizer or aged manure will work, too.

Let the sun do the work

Here's a labor-saving way to reclaim gardening space from an overgrown area. Lop off tall vegetation, drape a sheet of black plastic over the area, and anchor the edges with rocks. After about a month, the sun's heat will kill plants and weed seeds, and the area will be ready for rototilling.

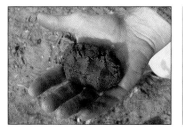

A fistful of clay soil squeezes into a tight, gummy ball when moist. It's sticky and hard to work.

Loam soil molds to the shape of your hand when it's moist, but when poked it will easily break apart.

Sandy soil is loose and crumbly. It feels gritty and won't hold any shape when you squeeze it.

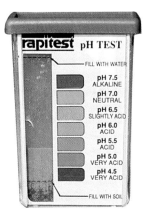

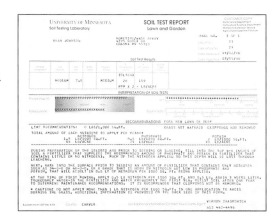

Read the results of a home soil test (left) by comparing the color of the liquid to the chart on each vial. For a complete soil analysis (right), mail your soil sample to a state agricultural agency, the country extension service, a university laboratory, or a commercial testing service.

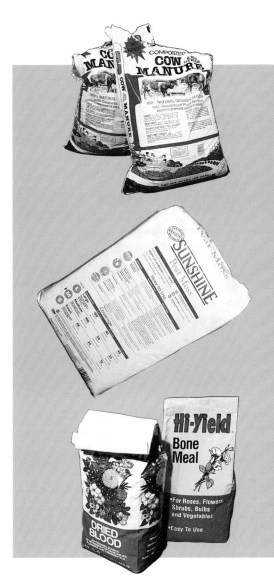

Soil amendments

Why	What to add	How much
To decrease soil acidity (pH) by 1.0	Hydrated lime	50 lbs. per 1,000 sq. ft. of sandy soil 70 lbs. per 1,000 sq. ft. of loam 80 lbs. per 1,000 sq. ft. of clay
To increase soil acidity (pH) by 1.0	Sulfur (if you use aluminum sulfate, read package directions for application rates)	8 lbs. per 1,000 sq. ft. of sandy soil 17 lbs. per 1,000 sq. ft. of loam 25 lbs. per 1,000 sq. ft. of clay
To increase acidity, add organic matter, and retain moisture	Peat moss	4 cu. ft. per 1,000 sq. ft.
To improve soil's friability	Organic matter (compost, peat moss, straw, aged manure)	2-3 inches over entire planting area, rototilled in, repeated annually
To boost soil nutrients	Complete fertilizer containing nitrogen (N), potassium (P), and phosphorus (K)	As directed, or 2 lbs. per 100 sq. ft.

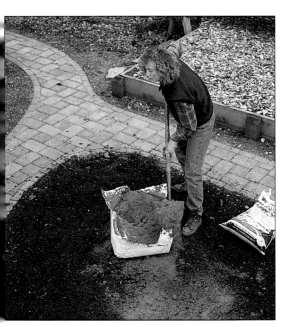

Spread amendments *evenly, then thoroughly mix them into the soil with a fork, shovel, or rototiller. The goal is to get the amendments well under the surface where they will do the most good.*

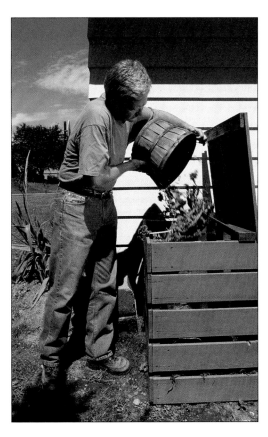

Make compost *with equal amounts of green and brown plant materials. Don't put in clippings from diseased plants. The disease may survive the heat of the compost pile and be spread to your other plants with the finished compost.*

The rototiller is a heavy machine that packs a lot of power. When you rent one, be sure you don't get a machine that's too big for you to manage. Even rototillers weighing less than 25 pounds can exert sub-

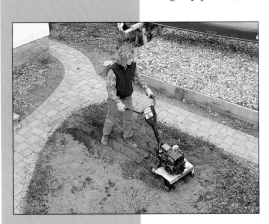

stantial force, both forward and up and down. Ask the rental folks to show you how to start it and stop it. Here are some additional safety tips.

Don't take too deep a bite at one time. If the tiller tends to bounce, or if it labors, ease up and make a second pass.

Wear heavy boots with good treads to be sure you can maintain your footing.

If a rock, root, or plant stem jams between the tiller tines, shut off the tiller and knock out the object with a stick – not with your hand.

Preparing the Soil

Roots can't penetrate hard, compacted soil, so start by breaking up and turning over the soil one shovelful at a time. Once you've turned over the soil by hand, use a rototiller to break it up even more.

Soil should be damp – but not wet – for rototilling. To tell if the moisture content is right, pick up a handful of soil and squeeze it. If it forms a ball that comes apart when you lightly poke it, it's fine. If the soil doesn't crumble, it's too wet, and if it doesn't clump at all, it's too dry.

After rototilling, level the area with a rake. If possible, prepare planting beds and add amendments in the late fall, so the soil will be in prime shape by spring (though you will need to till it again before planting).

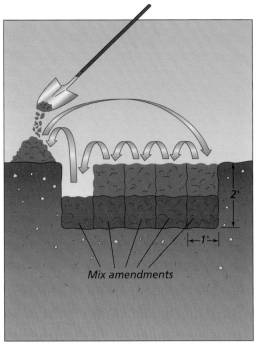

Mix amendments

Double digging *exposes the subsoil so it can be improved. Work your way across the bed, digging and moving 1-foot trenches of soil. Loosen and amend the exposed subsoil, but leave it in place. The soil from the last trench fills the first.*

Rototilled soil *is light, fluffy, and has a fine, uniform texture. There's no better way to work in organic matter and other amendments. Start tilling at a shallow depth, and make overlapping passes. This loosens the top layer of soil. Then reset the tiller to dig deeper until the top 8 inches of soil has been cultivated.*

Finishing the Edge

Garden edgings define a planting bed and keep plants in and grass out. You can buy edgings made of plastic, steel, or aluminum, or you can use pressure-treated lumber. Bricks and pavers are attractive, but grass and weeds tend to grow in the spaces between.

An alternative to using an edging material is to dig a simple beveled edge. With a flat-nosed shovel, make 4-inch-deep slices along the edge of the bed, forcing the soil back into the bed and leaving a gap between the bed and the lawn. Make the bevel slope at 45 degrees.

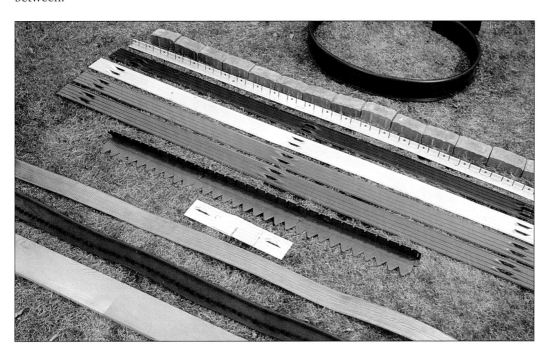

Edgings options *include wood, rubber, steel, plastic, aluminum, and vinyl. Vinyl edging is good for shaping sweeping curves. To make it easier to bend, warm it in the sun before installing it. For beds with sharp corners, consider wood or metal edging.*

1 **Set the edging** into the trench. The bead at the top should be level with the lawn soil. *Join sections with plastic connectors.*

2 **Drive stakes** through the edging from the planting bed side into the sod side. This anchors the edging.

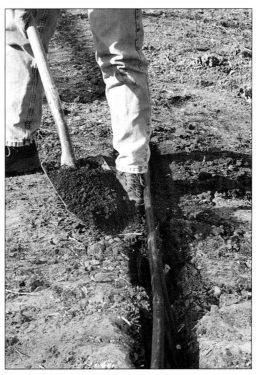

3 **Shovel the soil** back into the trench to cover up the edging sides and bottom. Tamp the soil firmly with your feet.

Weed killers

Edging, mulching, and weeding will keep your garden fairly free of grass and weeds. You'll have to decide for yourself whether you also want to use weed killers.

All chemical weed killers are different, so read the labels carefully to make sure the one you buy will kill weeds without harming your plants. Pre-emergent chemicals stop all seeds from germinating, including your flower and vegetable seeds. Post-emergent chemicals are used to kill mature weeds.

Carefully follow the manufacturer's directions for mixing and application. Wear a mask, gloves, and goggles, and don't spray when it's windy. Lock up weed killers where children can't get at them.

Mulch options

Bark nuggets *usually come from pine or cedar trees. It takes a lot of nitrogen to break down bark, so don't till it into the soil.*

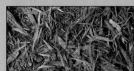

Shredded bark *clumps together, so it's better than bark nuggets on slopes.*

Leaves *increase soil acidity. Mulch with partially composted leaves, they are less likely to blow away.*

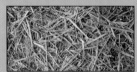

Straw *breaks down quickly, releasing its nutrients. It's good for holding seed and soil on a freshly seeded lawn.*

Gravel *(and other inorganic mulches) should be placed over landscape fabric to prevent the mulch from mixing into the soil.*

Rocks *come in a variety of colors and sizes and never break down. Weeds are likely to grow between them, but desirable plants may be difficult to start.*

Aged manure *is rich in nutrients, but may contain weed seeds. Don't use fresh manure because it could burn plant roots.*

Peat moss *is a good looking, but expensive mulch. It forms a water-absorbing mat which may keep roots from getting enough water.*

Grass clippings *break down quickly, so they're excellent for adding nutrients to a vegetable garden. To keep down weeds, lay newspaper under the clippings.*

Cocoa-bean hulls *look especially good in formal gardens. The hulls smell like chocolate for a couple of weeks after you spread them.*

Sawdust *looks good and breaks down slowly. You can probably get it free from a sawmill or millwork shop. Don't use sawdust from pressure-treated lumber.*

Shredded newspaper *decomposes very slowly and is inexpensive. It's best for utilitarian, rather than decorative, mulching.*

The Benefits of Mulch

Mulch keeps roots cool in hot weather and helps the soil hold moisture, so you can water less often. A 3- to 4-inch layer of mulch will also discourage weeds in planting beds. Organic mulches disintegrate over time, enriching the soil as they decompose. To keep rock and gravel mulches from sinking into the soil, place landscape fabric under the mulch.

Cover the soil *with a 3- to 4-inch layer of mulch, raking it out evenly. Most mulches are available by the bagful, but if you need a lot, it's cheaper to order a bulk delivery from a landscape supplier.*

Never use plastic sheeting as a substitute for landscape fabric in a planting bed, because it won't let water flow through to plant roots. You can use it to keep down weeds on garden paths, just make sure to punch a few drainage holes.

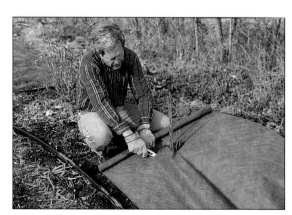

Unroll the landscape fabric, *then cut out the planting holes with a knife. Overlap rows of fabric by about an inch. Cover the fabric with several inches of mulch.*

TREES and SHRUBS

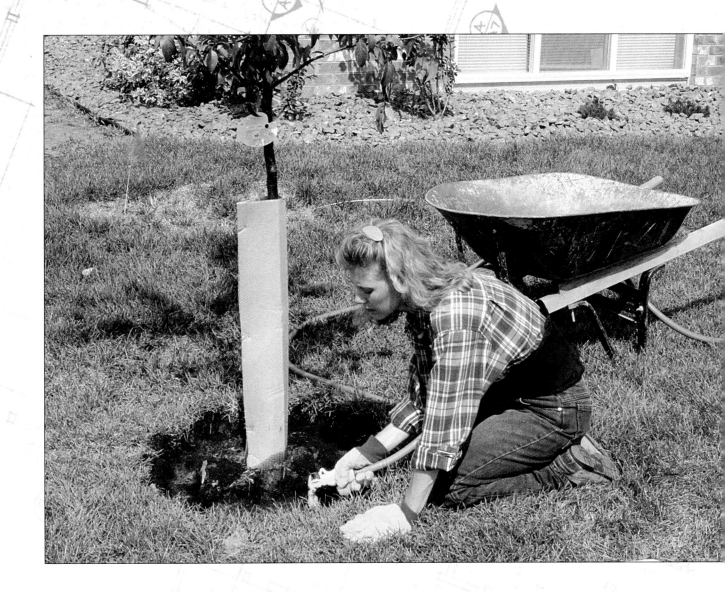

When you plant trees and shrubs, *you beautify your view during all four seasons and give your home powerful curb appeal. These plants serve other practical purposes, too. You can use them to create privacy from the street and neighboring yards, to create an outdoor living space, to screen off an ugly outbuilding or other eyesore, or to buffer your property against street noise, sun, or chilly winter winds. When planning changes to your landscape, work from the biggest (and most expensive) types of plants down to the smallest. Start with shade trees because they take the longest to grow. Add full-sized evergreens and ornamentals, then top off the plan with a variety of dwarf evergreens and flowering shrubs.*

Selecting Trees and Shrubs

The variety of trees and shrubs to choose from is overwhelming, no matter where you live. Your planning objectives, climate, and yard size will help you narrow the choices.

If you have trouble imagining what the plants will look like in your yard, work out the plan with pictures. Order duplicate catalogs from nurseries. Save one for reference and cut out the pictures of plants you like from the other. Move the cutouts around on your landscape diagram to experiment with different plant combinations and placements.

The climate in your area pretty much determines what you can grow. Remember to check USDA zone numbers, which range from 1 (coldest) to 10. These numbers indicate the regions where certain plants do best. Your neighborhood nursery is a good place to find plants that are suited to local conditions and will thrive in your soil type. Different soils present different challenges, but there are trees and shrubs available to meet them all.

Trees

When picking a tree you need to consider its height and spread at full maturity. The size of the trees should be in proportion to your yard and home. This will prevent the trees from overwhelming the property and eventually engulfing your other plants, and your home, in shade. For smaller yards, there are plenty of dwarf varieties available – whether you're choosing a deciduous tree (one that loses its leaves in fall) or an evergreen.

Shrubs

Shrubs are less expensive than trees. Even so, they represent major landscape purchases. Select them with care. Like trees, shrubs can be either deciduous or evergreen. They come in thousands of varieties featuring attractive foliage, flowers, interesting bark, or eye-catching fall and winter color.

Use shrubs as backdrops in flower beds, for ground covers, to attract birds, as part of a foundation planting, or anywhere in the landscape you want a visual lift. In general, mixed groups of shrubs look more natural than mass plantings of the same shrub. To give your yard a unified appearance, repeat a few of the shrubs in groupings throughout the yard.

Big, spreading trees like sugar maples, which can tower to 120 feet, belong on big lots. Smaller, brilliantly colored Japanese maples fit comfortably into even the tiniest yards.

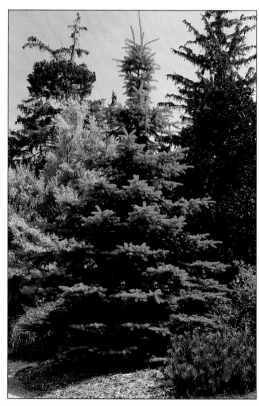

Evergreens splash color across drab winter landscapes. Southern gardeners will have fewer choices of coniferous evergreens, such as this Colorado spruce, but an abundance of broad-leaved evergreens.

How to locate a tree for shade

The best trees for shade are the ones with broad crowns. Plant them at least 15 feet from the house and at least 10 feet from driveways, walkways, and patios to keep the roots from lifting your pavement and invading your foundation. To create a shady spot for summer afternoons, plant the tree 10 to 15 feet south and 20 feet west of where you want the shade centered. Make sure to keep tall trees well away from power and telephone lines.

Small ornamental trees, such as flowering crab apples, typically have light, airy foliage and open branches. They're good for anchoring the ends of a planting bed or for providing the front yard with a focal point.

Apple trees and other small fruiting and flowering species add height and texture to a flower border. However, if you want a crop of edible apples, be prepared to spray against insects and disease.

Coniferous evergreen shrubs bear cones. They may have a rounded, upright, or spreading shape. Spreading conifers work well in rock gardens and as ground covers.

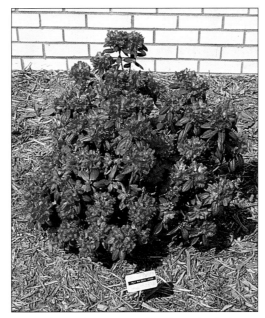

Broad-leaved evergreens, like these rhododendrons, often combine showy flowers with glossy, dark-green leaves that are attractive even after the blossoms fade.

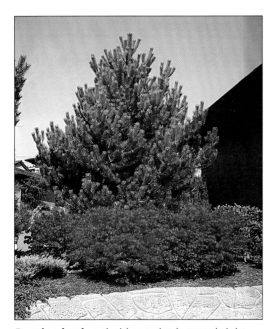

Burning bush, a deciduous shrub, turns bright red in late fall. It makes a big splash of color, but can grow too large without vigilant pruning.

Forsythia bushes can be trimmed into formally shaped hedges or left to grow as they please. Their golden blossoms are often first to open in early spring.

New construction *leaves a blank canvas for land-scaping. Before planting, define what you want to accomplish. Consider goals such as creating shade, privacy, a windbreak, or a focal point for your yard or garden.*

Ornamental trees, *such as flowering cherry, put on a beautiful show in the spring. They have a round shape and seldom grow more than 25 feet high. Ornamentals are best used as accents or focal points in the yard or garden.*

A large shade tree *planted on the same spot shades the house and helps block the view of neighboring houses. Heights range from 30 to 80 feet and more, depending on the species. Shapes include arching, rounded, pyramid, and columnar.*

A tall evergreen *makes a dense triangle of shade. It adds shade and color in all seasons. Densely needled evergreens make good wind and privacy screens. The soil under pine trees is highly acidic because of the fallen needles.*

Finer points of trees and shrubs

Looking for something special in a tree or shrub? Here are some characteristics to consider:

Winter interest

Look beyond evergreens. Plants with textured bark or bold branching shapes are especially dramatic in winter. Some good choices are birches, dogwoods, chokecherries, and sumacs. Some plants, like holly and barberry, retain colorful red berries throughout the winter.

Fragrance

Plant shrubs with fragrant flowers near windows or around outdoor living spaces, if possible, so their fragrance will fill your patio and house. Try Russian olive trees, lilacs, viburnums, and star magnolias.

Fruit

Apples, cherries, plums, and other fruits come in dwarf varieties that still grow full-size fruits. Remember that whatever you don't harvest will end up on the ground for you to clean up.

Texture

To avoid monotony, shoot for a variety of foliage types. Little leaves contrast nicely with broad ones, and wispy, feathery foliage can offset plants with large, coarse leaves.

Color

Shrubs come in many shades of green, so you can add visual depth to a planting bed by choosing dark-green shrubs for the back and plants with lighter-colored foliage for the front. With flowering shrubs, try to coordinate the bloom times for continuous color from spring through fall.

Smog tolerance

Urban landscapers often do well with ash, cedar, and cypress trees, which can withstand pollution. Ginkgo trees perform well, too.

Growth habits

Neatniks may want to avoid catalpas, whose long seedpods can quickly accumulate on a lawn. Likewise, female ginkgo trees drop messy, bad-smelling fruit. By contrast, male ginkgoes are easy to care for. They drop their leaves all at once, sometimes within minutes.

Hedges

Tall hedges provide a privacy screen from neighborhood activity and noise. They can define areas for outdoor living, or disguise long, plain walls or unattractive areas in the yard. A border of low shrubs works well to mark boundaries between properties, enclose flower beds, or direct traffic flow around the yard.

Hedges should be wider at the bottom than at the top; otherwise, the weight of water and snow on the upper branches is liable to break them. A wide base also provides good sun exposure for lower branches; this promotes leaf growth through the entire plant and encourages a full shape.

Formal hedges look solid. They are characterized by orderly lines and perfect geometric forms. Frequent pruning is required to keep them looking good. If you're not up to all that pruning, choose a less labor-intensive hedge to match an informal house.

An informal hedge, like this spirea, can be kept in bounds with moderate pruning. You can build informality into your hedge by planting in a zigzag pattern instead of in a straight line.

Shrubs for hedges

A hedge is nothing more than a grouping of shrubs planted so close together that they form an unbroken line.

Boxwood shrubs are often sheared into globes, rectangular shapes, and topiary forms.

Space male and female *Ilex* (holly) plants close together to ensure lots of berries.

Cypress, juniper, and arborvitae varieties come in shades of yellow, gray, blue, and deep green. Some tend to lose their middle leaves and lower branches as they age.

Bare-Root Stock

Bare-root trees and shrubs look like bunches of twigs. The plants are field-grown, then dug up during dormancy and sold at the beginning of the growing season. You can knock about a third off your landscaping bill by buying bare-root stock. The plants may look a little straggly the first season, but will look fine by the second year.

Try to get bare-root plants in the ground fast. When you get the plants, soak their roots overnight to help the plants break dormancy, then get them in the ground. Water them in with B-vitamin solution (sold at nurseries) after planting; this helps prevent shock and encourages root growth. If you have to wait a few days to plant, snip the strings binding the foliage, keep the plants lightly covered, and water them once or twice a day.

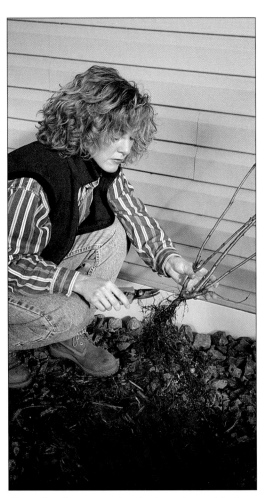

1 *Prune* branches lightly before planting trees and shrubs to help reduce transplanting shock. Dig the hole 6 inches deeper and wider than the plant's roots.

2 *Trim the roots* of each plant about ¼ inch to promote new growth. Also remove any damaged or broken roots. For clean cuts, use bypass pruners, not anvil pruners.

3 *Support the roots* on a mound of dirt in the bottom of the hole. The plant's crown (the point where the roots start) should be just above ground level, or 2 to 4 inches higher if you'll be mulching. Fill the hole halfway with soil, water, add the rest of the soil, then water again.

Container-Grown Stock

When you buy container-grown plants, look for healthy leaves that don't show signs of drastic pruning. Try to slip the container part-way off so you can inspect the roots. Roots on the surface of the soil and roots that encircle the plant are signs of a root-bound plant that may be difficult to transplant.

When removing a plant from its container, it's essential that the soil stay intact around the root ball. To release small plants, place your hand over the root ball, tip the container upside down, and gently pull the container off the plant. Lay a large container on its side, tap in several places, then slide the container off the root ball.

Transplanting large trees

Is it worth moving a tree? It depends in part on how much the tree would cost to replace. Also, not all trees transplant well. Your best success will probably be with younger softwoods and early-blooming varieties. Transplanting lowers a tree's overall resistance for about two years, so stay on guard against pests and disease during that time.

1 **Score the roots** with 4 or 5 vertical cuts to encourage them to grow outward rather than around in circles the way they tend to do in pots. Cut off encircled, tangled, or broken roots.

2 **Position the plant** and fill the hole halfway with soil.

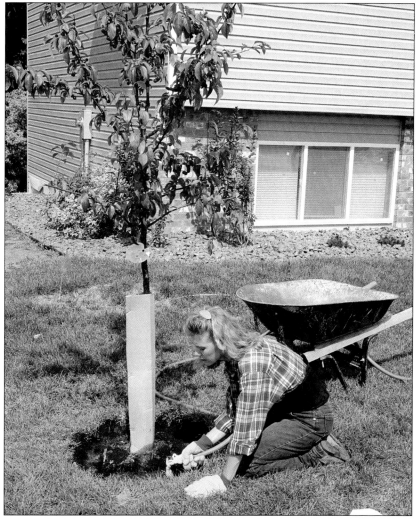

3 **Water thoroughly**, then top off the hole with more soil and water again. After planting, build a dirt moat over the rootball to help direct water to the roots. The walls of the moat should be about 4 to 5 inches high.

Transpalnting Shrubs

Most established shrubs can be moved from one place to another. To keep the roots moist, and to help soil adhere to the root ball, thoroughly water the shrubs two or three days before moving them. To minimize the amount of time the roots are exposed to air, dig the new holes before you lift the plants out of the old ones. Make the holes large enough to allow for a 6-inch gap all around the roots. A 5-foot evergreen and its root ball weigh about 150 pounds, so get someone to help you lever it out of the ground.

Settle the transplanted shrub in its new home the same way you would settle a newly purchased shrub. Water daily for the first two weeks.

1 *Tie the branches* into a bundle to keep them out of the way. Cut a shallow outline of the root ball in the soil, then dig down about 18 inches to get as many of the bottom roots as possible.

2 *Lever up* one side of the shrub in the hole and lay in the burlap, bunching it up as much as possible under the shrub. Then raise the other side and pull the burlap through.

3 *Tie the burlap* to keep the root ball intact during the move. Drag the shrub to its new home on a piece of cardboard or plastic. Set the shrub in the hole, then trim away all exposed burlap.

Propagating shrubs

If you need more shrubs than the budget allows, try propagating your own. The method you use depends on the type of shrub: take cuttings from the new growth of deciduous shrubs, layer either deciduous or evergreen shrubs, divide any shrub that produces branches from underground buds.

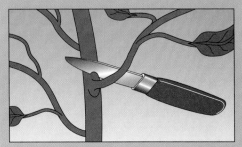

Take cuttings by slicing 8-inch shoots from the shrub's new growth. Make the cut with one V-shaped pass from the top and another from the bottom. Leave a sliver of parent wood (called a heel) attached to the cutting. Trim the cutting to just above the first bud, then pot the heel in seed-starting soil.

To divide a shrub, dig it out of the ground, then fork, spade, or shear it into two or more pieces. Make sure each section gets a fair share of vigorous roots. A shrub should be at least three years old before you divide it.

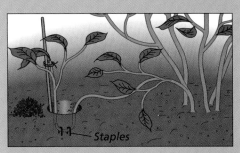

In layering, you bend a branch so that a 12-inch shoot remains, peel off the leaves, then twist the branch to break the outer coating. Anchor the branch in a shallow hole, then support the branch with a stake and backfill with soil.

Maintaining Trees and Shrubs

An occasional pruning will help keep trees and shrubs attractive and healthy. Look at the plant from several angles and pinpoint your goals. Do you want to reshape the plant? Open up the center? Raise the crown? Reduce its size? Whatever your goals, always remove dead and crossing branches. Pay attention to timing, too. Prune spring-flowering plants after the blossoms die. Summer-flowering plants should be pruned in late spring, before new growth begins. If in doubt, ask a local nursery or the country extension agent for advice.

Direct water right to the roots of thirsty trees with a water lance, or root waterer. This device attaches to a hose and spikes into the ground. Use it every few feet around the drip zone.

Wrapping the trunk of a new tree helps protect the delicate bark from nicks and bruises, insect and animal damage, and sun scald. Use either tree wrap especially designed for this purpose or burlap strips. Remove the wrap when it begins to disintegrate (usually about a year).

Fertilize trees every spring and fall once they're established to keep them growing vigorously. You can scratch the fertilizer in with a hand cultivator or use a liquid food.

Three stakes will support a young tree. Drive them well beyond the root system, and loosely attach the ties to the trunk. Gentle swaying will help strengthen the trunk.

Waste not

Garden-size chipper/shredders let you grind yard waste to a fine mulch you can use to top off planting beds or feed to the compost pile. Small electric models usually are limited to branches measuring under 2 inches in diameter, but

gas-driven types can process material up to 3 or 4 inches. Always wear ear and eye protection when running one of these machines. Never reach into the feed hopper or discharge chute of a running machine.

Pruning Pointers

The purpose of pruning is to promote healthy growth, to constrain the size of a tree or to lift its crown, to promote leaf growth by admitting air and sunlight, and to remove damaged branches.

- Start shaping trees when they're young. It's easier than trying to reshape an old tree that has grown out of bounds.
- Prune whole branches to let air and light into the middle of the plant. Nibbling the tips of the branches promotes thick growth on the outside of the plant, none at the center.
- Some trees respond best to pruning in the spring, some in the fall or winter, and some can handle it any time. Pruning some species at the wrong time can make them more susceptible to insects and disease (oak wilt, for example). Check with a local nursery or your county extension office if you're not sure what to prune when.

- Water sprouts look harmless, but they can suck strength from the tree. Clip these soft, fast-growing shoots flush with the trunk or branch.
- Suckers grow from the bottom of the trunk or from the roots. Dig down to where they attach, and nip them off flush.
- Rubbing branches can damage bark, allowing pests and disease to flourish. Prune off one branch, then cut the damaged part off the other.
- When sawing branches, make the first cut 6 to 12 inches away from the trunk. Cut upward from the bottom of the branch for about one-third of its thickness. Then move an inch closer to the trunk and cut downward. This maneuver prevents the bark from ripping. Finally, remove the stub that remains.
- Prune close to the trunk, but stay outside the growth collar at the base of the branch.

3-year renewal cycle for shrubs

Before. This overgrown shrub probably wouldn't survive the drastic pruning it needs if you were to do it all at once, but it can be rejuvenated by following a three-year pruning cycle.

Year 1. Cut a third of the branches and stems right back to the base. Focus on removing the thickest, woodiest, and oldest ones.

Year 2. Remove another third of the branches, again concentrating on thick, woody, and old growth. Don't touch new growth.

Year 3. Lop off the last third of the old branches, leaving all new growth intact. Each following year, remove old growth as needed, cutting out the oldest third and leaving the youngest, most productive branches.

Before

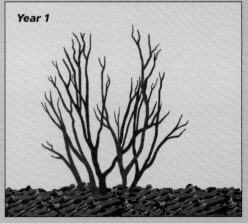

Year 1

Year 2

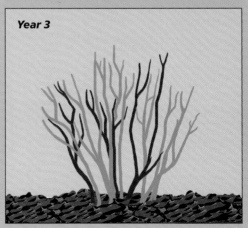

Year 3

PATIOS and WALKWAYS

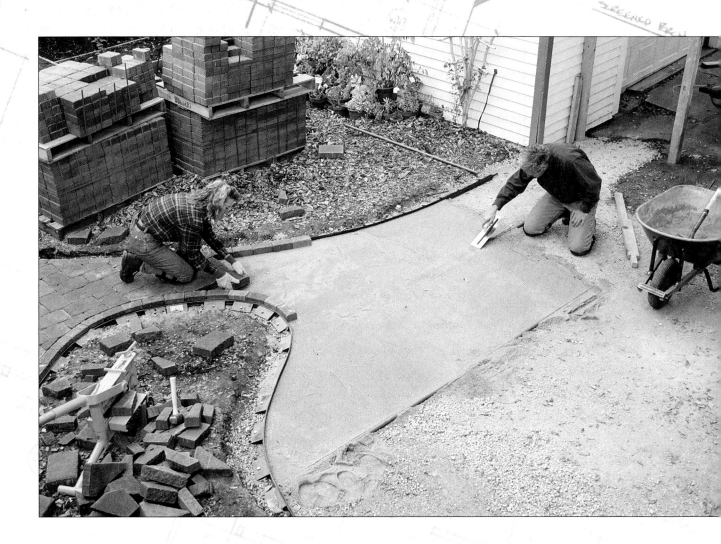

Concrete pavers, bricks, and paving stones can be laid in either of two ways: bedded in loose sand, or set in mortar and concrete. While concrete is hard and durable, it's not the best choice for most backyard projects. Frost heaves can make it buckle and crack, and it's difficult to repair or rearrange. That's why we prefer to set them in sand. The pavers may settle a bit, but they stay put and they don't crack. And you can dig them up and rearrange the layout when you want to enlarge that flower bed or move the patio farther into the sunshine.

Concrete Pavers

Because they are man-made, concrete pavers offer a lot of choices for colors and shapes. Brick-shaped pavers fit together in regular geometric patterns. Assortments of square and rectangular blocks make it easy to construct regular borders around a center field of pavers arranged in a more complex pattern. Pavers also come as hexagons and other interlocking shapes.

Unlike bricks, pavers aren't uniformly square-edged. The top may have rounded edges, like an old cobblestone, while little ribs on the sides prevent the pavers from being set tight together. This is important because there has to be some room for sand in between them. Even though the sand never solidifies like concrete, it does settle into a tight matrix that locks the pavers in place.

Planning the layout

Whatever pattern you choose, check it out with the actual pavers before you start to dig. Assemble some pavers and measure the ac-

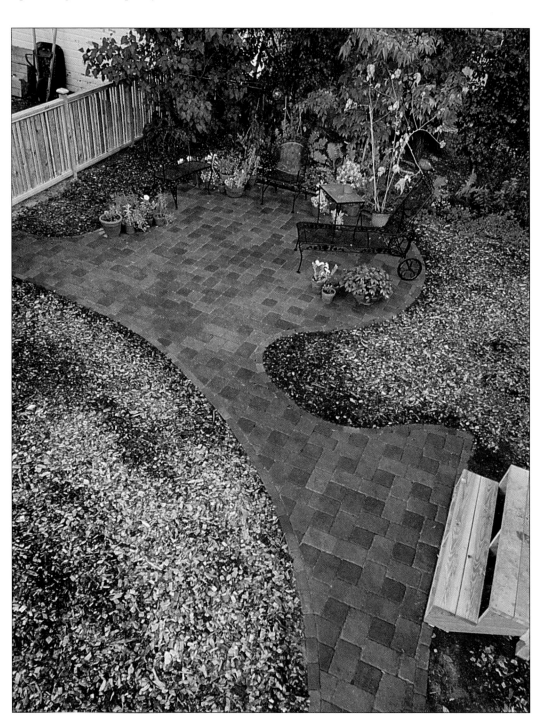

Pavers can be laid in rectangular patterns or in freeform shapes. As with all dry-laid masonry, a good bed of gravel and sand is the key to success.

tual space they occupy. Then adjust the shape of your walkway or patio to use only whole pavers. Getting it wrong means trimming pavers to fit along the edges.

Use an old hose to outline the walk and patio on the ground. You need room to work, so shift the hose about 6 inches bigger than the finished size. Remember, the more curves and irregular shapes in your layout, the more pieces you'll have to cut, which can take a lot of time. When you're happy with the layout, spray-paint the outline along the hose onto the grass or soil.

Preparing the base

The key to a successful paver patio is a stable base of gravel topped with coarse sand. The gravel has to be compacted to a finished depth of 3 to 4 inches, with the sand an inch thick. Since the pavers themselves are 2 inches thick, you have to dig out to a total depth of 6 to 7 inches. Subsoils of wet clay or silt may need a deeper base, as will heavy-duty installations such as driveways. If you think there's a need to stabilize the soil, spread a layer of geotextile fabric across the excavation before you start to add gravel.

Basket weave. *This simple, two-by-two layout is easy to set and finish. Unlike some paver patterns, this one can be completed without cutting the edge pavers.*

Running bond. *Each row is offset by half the length of a paver, same as in a brick wall. You'll need to buy or cut half-pavers to complete the layout.*

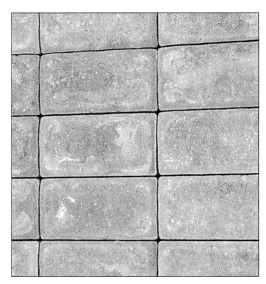

Jack-on-jack. *Because it is so regular, the jack-on-jack layout requires very precise spacing. It doesn't interlock as tightly as other patterns.*

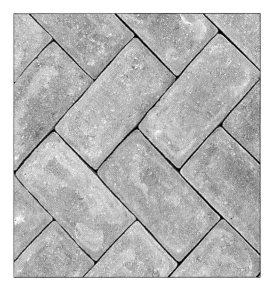

Herringbone. *The herringbone pattern creates triangular spaces along the edges, so it requires cutting a lot of pavers to finish.*

You say class 2, I say ...

Class 2 gravel, ¾-inch minus, AB3. 21A, and ¾-inch crusher run – all refer to the same grade of gravel.

Whatever they call it, a suitable base for walkways and patios should contain a uniform mix of pieces ranging from ¾ inch down to fine particles. Ask your supplier what local contractors generally use and how deep they compact it, then follow their lead.

Gravel generally compacts to about half its starting mass, plus you need some extra to fill in holes. A cubic yard of ¾-inch minus gravel is enough for about 80 square feet of 3-inch base.

Work out the grade as you dig, to make sure the paving doesn't direct water toward the house. The grade should slope away from the house at the rate of 1 inch per 4 running feet, or 2%, more or less. Move earth to change the lay of the land at the start of the project – don't leave it for later – though you can fine-tune the slope while raking out the gravel.

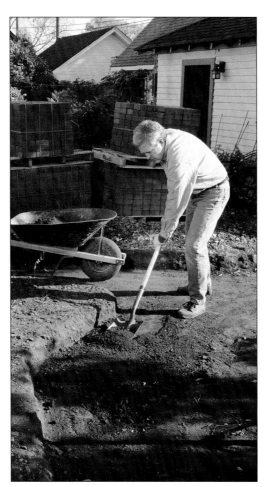

1 *Dig out the pathway* to a depth of 6 inches. Skim the high spots off the base with a flat shovel. Try not to disturb the earth in the bottom of the hole, except to remove large rocks. Fill in any holes with gravel.

2 *Rake a 4-inch layer* of gravel into the excavation. Compact the first layer, then add a second layer and compact it as well. Each layer of gravel compacts to about half its starting thickness.

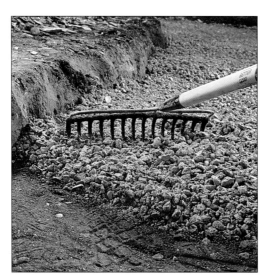

3 *Tease the gravel* into a smooth bed with the rake. This limestone gravel is ¾-inch minus with fines, which means the pieces go from ¾ inch down to dust. To compact well, the gravel should be moist, but not wet.

4 *Compact the gravel* with a gas-powered compactor. It makes a lot of noise, so wear hearing protection. You'll use the same machine again later on to settle the pavers and to pack sand between them.

5 ***Slope the gravel*** *so the patio will carry water away from the house. Adjust the slope by adding gravel on the high side and digging deeper on the low side. Don't make grade by skimping on gravel or by adding extra sand because the pavers are liable to settle too much.*

6 ***Scrape the sand level*** *by running a notched screed board on the plastic edging. Notch the screed board to create the desired depth of the sand bed, usually 1 inch.*

Setting the edging

Plastic edging is stable and easy to work with. It keeps the pavers in place, and it has an inside lip that locks it into the sand bed. The edging also establishes the reference surface for screeding the sand. Use rigid pieces to edge straight sections; special segmented edging goes around curves.

To set the edging, re-mark the layout with the old hose or with stakes and string. Plug the edging pieces together end-to-end on the layout lines. Nail the edging to the base of compacted gravel with 10-inch galvanized landscape spikes.

7 ***A one-inch pipe*** *guides the screed board toward the middle of the patio. Spread the sand with the wheelbarrow, shovel, and rake before leveling it off with the screed board.*

8 ***Screed between a pair of pipes*** *out in the middle of the patio. Move the pipes from place to place to level the entire patio. Remove the pipes when you're done, and trowel sand into the tracks they leave behind.*

Cutting pavers

There's a knack to splitting pavers with a brick chisel and mallet, but it's not difficult to learn. Draw the cut line with chalk. Place the paver on the bed of sand, and set the chisel on the line. Hit the chisel with a fist maul. You don't have to drive the hammer, just lift it about 18 inches above the chisel and let it drop. If the paver doesn't break cleanly, straighten the cut by chipping it with the chisel and hammer. With practice, you'll learn how each kind of paver breaks so you can make an edge that doesn't need much finishing.

9 *A hydraulic splitter speeds things up when you have lots of pavers to cut. Set the paver under the blade, then pull the handle down. Press down on the keeper side of the stone to make the break slope away from the top surface. Rub the cut edges together to smooth off rough areas.*

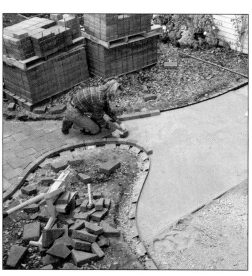

11 *You can't walk on the sand after screeding, so screed a bit, set the pavers, then screed some more. Kneeling on the pavers while you work helps settle them into the sand.*

Caring for pavers

Pavers may develop a white, powdery efflorescence on their surface, and they might even come with it. Efflorescence is a mineral that migrates out of the concrete. Though it may not look great, it doesn't affect the strength or durability of the pavers. You can buy cleaning products formulated specifically for removing efflorescence from concrete.

10 *Fill in the edges with pieces of pavers cut to·fit. Draw the cutting lines on the pavers with chalk so you can see the marks. This cut-and-fit process can take a lot longer than setting the field pavers.*

12 *Work out from an edge and work in easy stages. Place each paver tight against its neighbors, allowing the built-in nibs to set the spacing.*

Pavers can be sealed to enhance their color, prevent efflorescence, and resist stains. Use a sealer designed for pavers, not an all-purpose material. The sealer probably will have to be reapplied every couple of years.

Freeze-thaw cycles may crack a paver, as will zealous compacting. Pry out the broken paver and replace it. Be sure to brush sand all around the new paver.

13 ***Settle the pavers*** *into the sand with the compactor, then throw a light layer of sand over the whole area. Sweep it into the joints, then go over the pavers with the compactor to vibrate the sand into a tight pack.*

Veneer Pavers Over Concrete

A veneer of pavers conceals the industrial look of poured concrete. The pavers go directly on top of the concrete, but it must be smooth and even with a neatly troweled finish. Border pavers are glued in place with masonry adhesive, and so are steps and risers. Broad areas of field pavers are laid dry – the glued border and sanded joints will keep them in place.

1 ***Set the risers.*** *Regular pavers (right) make an attractive riser. Lay out the pavers so the treads overhanging the risers by ½ inch. Glue them down with masonry adhesive, which works best on dry and dust-free surfaces. Split-face block risers (left) contrast with the color and texture of the paver treads, which makes it easier to see the individual steps. Wooden shims in the lower course position the risers and treads, and keep the adhesive from squeezing out of the joint.*

2 ***Perimeter pavers*** *aren't retained by any edging, so they must be glued to the concrete base with masonry adhesive. Make sure there's no stray grit to interfere with a good bond.*

3 ***Dry-set the field pavers.*** *These lifting tongs take some of the back-breaking work out of it. The field pavers will stay in place without any adhesive, once you sweep sand between them to keep them from shifting.*

4 ***Use a mason's line*** *and a spacing tool to align the pavers. Make the joint lines as straight and regular as you can.*

5 ***Sweep medium-grain sand*** *into the joints between pavers. Sweep hard in all directions to force sand down into the joints. Don't run a compactor over pavers set on concrete – they'll crack.*

Setting Flagstones

A flagstone path is less formal than a paver walkway. Flagstones vary in thickness, from 1½ inches up to about 2 inches. One ton of flagstones will cover about 100 square feet. The basic method of installation is the same as pavers, but there are several important differences.

Flagstones need a compacted bed of crushed limestone gravel at least 3 inches thick, topped with a layer of uncompacted gravel instead of sand. Fit the irregular stones together like a jigsaw puzzle. The stones can touch, or the spaces can be as wide as 2 or 3 inches. And you can always break or cut stones to fit. Trowel loose gravel under the stones to make them sit level. Complete the paving by brushing fine gravel into the joints.

1 **Set flagstones** in a layer of loose gravel over a 3-inch bed of compacted gravel. Level each stone by troweling loose gravel underneath it. Make sure each stone sits flat and level with its neighbors.

2 **Bring plastic edging** up to the flagstones and nail it to the earth with 10-inch galvanized landscape spikes. The edging holds the stones in place and keeps the gravel base from spreading. Segmented edging flexes to follow the irregular shapes.

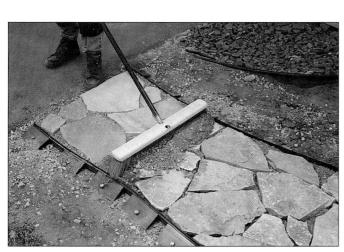

3 **Brush fine gravel** into the joints between the flagstones. This crushed black granite contrasts with the light color of the stones.

It doesn't take long before grass sprouts between the flagstones. You can pull it out and brush in more crushed stone, or leave it for an informal look.

Make Your Own Paving Stones

You can make your own concrete paving stones. The concrete is poured right in place, using a special form. The form is divided into sections, so the finished pavement looks like an intricate pattern of fit stones. This method gives you control over color and surface finish, and it is somewhat cheaper than working with real stone. The basic method is to make and finish a square and then to move on to the next while the concrete is still wet. For best results, stay with earth colors – shades of red and brown.

1 ***Add the color*** *to the concrete mix. Measure carefully because the mix has to be firm enough to hold its shape after you pull off the form. You'll need to mix many batches to complete a patio of any size.*

Practice pours pay off

We discovered that you can get good looking results with these forms, but only if you don't cut any corners. We also learned that it pays to pour a couple of practice forms and to experiment with color and finishing techniques before you start on the project itself. Be sure to work the surface with the pointing trowel to bury every trace of aggregate. Exposed aggregate destroys the illusion of colored stone.

2 ***Set the form in place*** *on a 2-inch bed of compacted gravel topped with smooth sand. The forms are designed to fit neatly together and they're sized to receive an 80-pound bag of concrete mix, regular or fiber-reinforced. Pack mixed concrete into the form.*

3 ***Lift the form*** *off the wet concrete, then use a mason's pointing trowel to clean up the edges. Work the top surface and edges of each section to force all of the aggregate below the surface.*

4 ***Stipple the surface*** *with a coarse brush. Then leave the concrete alone to cure while moving on to the next pour.*

5 ***Brush sand*** *into the joints after the concrete has cured overnight.*

FENCES, ARBORS and TRELLISES

Arbors, trellises, and fences *are all relatively easy to build, and they will add a lot to the appeal, usefulness, and value of your property. Since you can put an arbor or a trellis just about anywhere, it also creates a destination – a focal point or a place to visit in your landscape. While a fence also has a variety of practical purposes (privacy, protection, weather control), its most important function probably is psychological. A fence divides the landscape into two parts: your yard, and the rest of the world.*

Wood Fences

Wood is the most common fencing material. Resistance to moisture and decay are top priorities when choosing the wood species. Redwood, cedar, and black locust are naturally rot-resistant, but pressure-treated pine is less expensive and more durable.

Talk before you build

In most areas, there are regulations about fence height and setbacks. Some communities also require a permit, so talk to your building department before you begin. If there is any chance of buried cables and pipes in your neighborhood, call your utility companies to mark them with spray paint. This is a free service in most places.

Good fences may make good neighbors, but the sudden appearance of a new fence also can cause hard feelings. Head off trouble with your neighbors (who might not like the idea of your fence as much as you do) by discussing your plans with them.

Don't guess about the property line. Look for the survey pins or have a new survey done. Then build the fence inside the property line, so you can maintain it without trespassing. Finally, face the good side of the fence toward the street or toward the neighbor's property – in many places this is required by code.

Fence layout

Start by making an accurate bird's-eye drawing of the area where you plan to build the fence. Note big rocks, trees, and other obstructions. If the site slopes or if there are any dramatic changes in grade, make an elevation drawing as well.

Many styles of fencing

Picket fences go with most architectural styles, but offer minimum privacy. You can shape the pickets and vary their height to suit your taste.

Free-form fences can convey any look you like. In this case, the fence repeats the shape of the house facade.

Vertical board fences provide partial privacy and buffer the wind, while allowing good air circulation. They're hard for kids to climb.

Stockade fences offer security, privacy, and weather control. They can appear overwhelming unless softened at the base with plantings.

Alternate board fences look good from both sides. They offer partial privacy and good air circulation.

Basketweave fences also have two finished sides. A tight weave is more private than an open weave, but restricts air flow.

Lattice fences offer varying degrees of privacy, depending on the tightness of the weave. They are often used to support climbing plants.

Rail fences are excellent for marking property boundaries. They're also inexpensive to build.

Locate the corner posts on your drawing, then space the line posts evenly between them (the posts should be no more than 8 feet apart). In northern climates the corner posts and gate posts should extend below the frost line, with line posts set in the ground about a third of their own height. In warmer climates, set all posts at least a third of the fence height in the ground.

Lay out the fence and mark the post locations using stakes and string. If the ground is flat, just pound a stake at each end of the fence and string a line between the stakes. Measure off post locations on the line until you get to the end of the fence. If the fence will travel down a slope, layout is a little more involved. Generally, steep slopes look better with stepped fences, while on long, gentle slopes, the fence can follow the land.

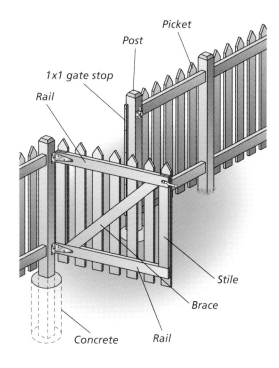

Picket
Post
1x1 gate stop
Rail
Stile
Brace
Rail
Concrete

Every fence consists of vertical posts set in the ground, connected by one or more horizontal rails. The fill-in material between the posts (in this case wooden pickets) is called screening.

Square the fence corners with the 3-4-5 method. From the corner, measure out 4 feet along the fence line and 3 feet along the house. Hold a tape diagonally between the marks. Move the line back and forth until the diagonal distance is exactly 5 feet.

Stake the position of the first post, then measure along the layout line to locate the rest of the posts. The line indicates the outside face of the posts, so you'll have to measure in from the string to find the center of each post. Mark the spots with stakes or ribbon.

Stepping the fence down a slope

To run a privacy fence down a steep slope, you have to step it so that each section is level. To lay out the sections, drive a stake at the top of the slope and another at the bottom. The bottom stake must be at least as tall as the top of the slope. Stretch a layout line between the bottom of the uphill stake and the top of the downhill stake, and adjust it to be perfectly level. Next, measure from the ground at the bottom stake up to the line, to determine the change in elevation. To figure the amount of step-down for each post, divide the change in elevation by the number of fence sections.

Drilling post holes

Digging fence posts is hard work. If the dirt is fairly loose, you can use a post-hole digger (also called a clamshell digger). The jaws of this double shovel open and shut, which allows you to scoop out the dirt. If your soil is hard, or you just want to get the job done more quickly, rent a power auger. They come in one- and two-person models. For really hard soil, rent both 8-inch and 12-inch bits. Use the 8-inch bit to prebore, then finish off with the 12-inch bit. Although a power auger dramatically cuts your digging time, it can be difficult to steer a straight hole.

1 *Rent a power auger* if you have lots of post holes to dig. Pull the auger up every now and then to clear dirt from the hole. If you hit a rock, try to dig it out with shovels and a clamshell digger. If the rock won't budge, move over 6 inches to try again.

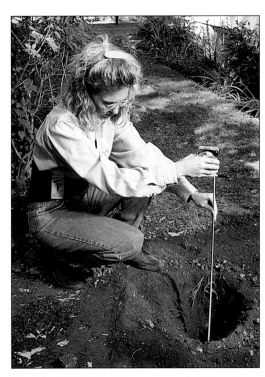

2 *Check hole depth* as you work, using a tape or a T-gauge made of 1x2s. Dig each hole at least a third the height of the fence; in northern climates, be sure to dig below the frost line, which may be 42 inches or even more.

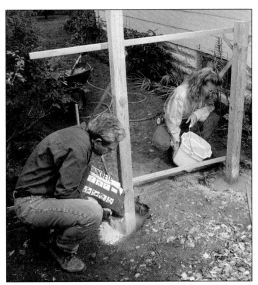

3 *Set and plumb* the end, corner, and gate posts first. Rotate the posts so their faces follow the line of the fence. Brace them with pieces of 2x4, then fill the holes with dry concrete mix, add water, and stir with a stick.

4 *Mound a dirt collar* around all the posts so that water will run off. Build up the soil in the post hole in 2-inch to 3-inch layers. Tamp each layer with a piece of 2x4 as you go.

Setting the posts

Always set corner, end, and gate posts in concrete. Line posts can also be set in concrete, but in areas with mild winters you can just fill the hole with gravel and top it off with soil.

We like to mix the concrete right in the post hole. Set the post on a few inches of gravel in the bottom of the hole, then plumb it and brace it. Then pour a sack of ready-mix concrete into the post hole, stopping several inches short of ground level. Add the amount of water specified by the instructions on the sack, stir with a stick, then leave it to cure for a couple of days. After the concrete has cured, fill the holes up the rest of the way with top soil mounded up to help drain water away from the posts.

There's a lot to keep track of when you're setting fence posts. They not only have to be vertical and the right distance apart, but their faces have to follow the line of the fence.

To align the post faces, restring the layout line after you dig the post holes. Then plumb each post with a level as you set it, making sure it is plumb in both directions. Then twist the post so the outside face touches the string from one edge to the other and check that it's still plumb.

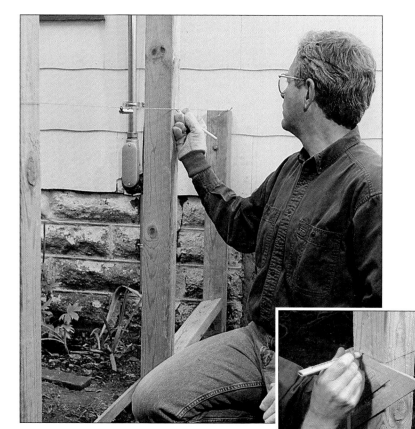

5 **Mark the height** of each post by stringing a level line from one end of the fence to the other. Mark where the line crosses each post.

6 **Transfer** the height mark all around the post with a speed square. This will help you keep the cut straight.

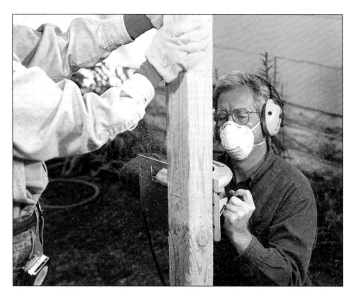

7 **Trim posts** to height with a circular saw, reciprocating saw, or handsaw. Cut 4x4 posts in two passes. To help them shed water, bevel the post tops or attach caps cut from 6x6 blocks. Wear a dust mask to avoid inhaling sawdust.

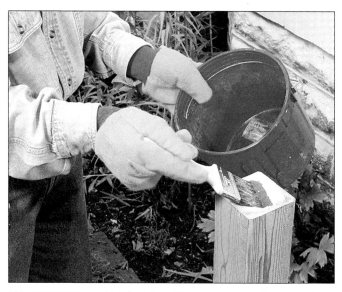

8 **Treat exposed end grain** with a generous coating of sealer-preservative. Even with pressure-treated lumber, the newly cut end grain is susceptible to decay.

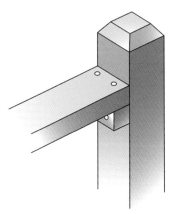

Butt and toenail joint

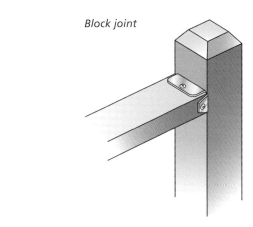

Block joint

Rail clips

Rails and screening

The rails connect the fence posts and support the fence-screening material. Exactly where the rails intersect the posts will depend on the style of your fence. The simplest way to attach rails to posts is with a butt joint reinforced by a wood block, toenails, rail clips, or angle brackets. You can also seat the rail ends in a cutout called a dado, but it takes skill to cut these joints and the process is time-consuming. However you choose to install the rails, check frequently to be sure they're level.

Vertical screening materials, such as pickets and boards, won't look good if they aren't plumb, so frequently check their alignment with a 4-foot level. As a general rule, don't let screening material overhang the top or bottom rail by more than 2 or 3 inches; otherwise, the unsupported ends are liable to warp.

1 ***To make a dado***, *saw the top and bottom edges and also make several intermediate cuts in between the layout lines. Make the cuts about an inch deep, and make sure they're all the same depth.*

2 ***Break up the waste wood*** *by levering against the saw cut with a sharp chisel.*

Fasten rails to posts *with 2½-inch or 3-inch galvanized nails. Drive the nails at angles to one another, which increases their holding power. Rail clips may require shorter nails, while angle brackets work best with galvanized screws.*

Angle bracket

3 *Knock the waste wood* out of the dado with a hammer and chisel. Pare the bottom of the dado down flat and smooth.

4 *Dado joints* have a finished look that you can't get with ordinary reinforced butt joints. Because they can bear a lot of weight, you can't beat dado joints when a fence design calls for heavy rails and screening.

5 *Use a spacer block* to make uniform spaces between pickets. If the space between screening boards is equal to the width of the boards themselves, just use a spare board for a spacer.

6 *Fasten each picket* with two nails at each rail. When you're nailing near the ends of the pickets, blunt the nail tips with a hammer or drill pilot holes to avoid splitting the wood.

Fasteners

Don't try to save money by skimping on nails. Cheap nails will loosen up and eventually bleed rust through the paint or stain. Double-dipped galvanized nails are best. In coastal locations, where fasteners have to endure salt air, invest in stainless steel. Although pricey, stainless steel nails are the most weather-resistant of all. They're also the only kind of nails that won't make a black streak on redwood. Deck nails, which have a twisted shank, resist popping better than common nails.

Gates

When designing a gate, make it wide enough for any lawn tractor or snow thrower that will need to travel through it. Since gates wider than 5 feet tend to sag, divide them into two sections that meet in the middle. Fences move with the weather, so always leave about ¼ inch of clearance between each side of the gate and the posts to make sure the gate swings freely.

Gates take a real pounding, so use large, corrosion-resistant hinges and long, non-rusting screws. Don't be afraid to overbuild big gates with larger hardware than seems necessary and plenty of bracing.

All wood gates should be strengthened with a diagonal brace. Run a wood brace from the top of the latch side to the bottom of the hinge side so it counteracts the tendency to sag. Attach a wire and turnbuckle brace in the opposite direction. Run it diagonally from the bottom of the latch side to the top of the hinge side, with the turnbuckle located in the middle.

Finally, supplement the latch mechanism with a wooden stop nailed to the post. The latch may work loose and fail, but the stop will guard the gate from the certain destruction of being shoved the wrong way through its opening.

1 *Fit the diagonal brace* in the gate frame and fasten it with screws. Check that the assembly is square. If the hinges mount onto the backside of the post, attach them to the gate now, while it's down flat.

2 *Prop up the gate*, aligning the gate bottom with the bottom of the fence. Establish the clearance between the gate and the posts with shims, which will also hold the gate in place while you fasten it. Plumb the gate before screwing the hinges to the post.

Finishing your fence

Finish a wood fence to keep it looking beautiful and boost its resistance to rot-causing fungi.

Clear, oil-based water-repellent sealers enhance the natural color and grain of the wood while protecting it from the weather. Recoat the fence every other year.

Stain comes in opaque and semi-transparent formulations. Opaque stain works like paint. It covers up much of the wood grain, but since it soaks into the pores of the wood, it won't flake off. Semi-transparent stain offers the same protection but lets more of the grain show through.

When painting exterior wood, always start with an oil-based primer. Then apply two coats of exterior wood-finish or oil- or latex-based paint.

Chain-Link Fence

When your goal is to keep children and pets inside the yard without spending a lot of money, you can't beat chain-link fence. Chain-link fences come in standard heights of 42 inches, 4 feet, 6 feet, and 8 feet. The mesh sizes and thicknesses vary, too: the smaller the mesh, the more expensive the fencing. If you have small children, choose a fence with small mesh, because it's harder for little feet to get a toehold. Thicker-gauge materials are more expensive than thinner gauge, and colored vinyl-coated fencing is more expensive than plain galvanized. To economize, you can combine vinyl and galvanized products in the same fence. Use the vinyl on parts of the fence that are visible from the street, and the galvanized at the back of the yard.

Chain-link fences are strong, economical to install, and virtually maintenance-free. Colored chain-link fences blend in with many yardscapes and complement a variety of architectural styles.

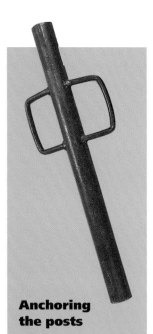

Anchoring the posts

Two-inch steel pipe is sturdy enough – and sharp enough – to be driven directly into the ground. A post driver is a weighted tube with handles and a sturdy end-cap. Slip the post driver over the post, position the post, then lift and drop the driver two or three times. Check for plumb, adjust as necessary, then hit the post another two or three times. Continue until the post is the right height.

A metal anchor holds the post in place. Dig down about 6 inches, slide the anchor shoe over the post, then drive the anchoring stakes diagonally into the ground. Once you tighten the anchor shoe's bolts onto the stakes and onto the post, it won't be going anywhere.

Installing chain-link fence

Chain-link fence posts are 2-inch galvanized pipe. There are two good ways to install the posts: they can be set in concrete, or they can be driven directly into the ground and locked in place with special anchoring hardware.

If you're using concrete, dig the post holes 3 feet deep. Make them 6 inches in diameter at the top and belled out a little wider at the

1 *Set terminal posts first whether using a shoe-and-anchor system (as shown here) or concrete. Pound the posts into the ground with a post driver.*

2 *Set the line posts next, attaching the layout line directly to the end posts. Space the posts evenly between fence sections, but no more than 10 feet apart.*

3 *Strip off a circle of sod at the base of each post. Dig down 6 inches, slip the shoe over the post, and slide it down into the hole.*

4 *Drive the anchor stakes into the ground with a heavy hammer. Set the line posts and mount the top rail before tightening any of the shoes.*

5 *Tightening down the shoes is a two-person job. One person looks down the line from the end of the fence; the other walks along it plumbing the posts and tightening the shoes.*

6 *Brace bands on the terminal post bolt to a fitting placed on the end of the top rail. Set the brace band 2 inches down from the top of the terminal post.*

bottom to prevent frost heave. Set the corner, gate, and end posts (called the terminal posts) first.

If you're using an anchor-type fence system, you can drive the posts to the height you need. Posts set in concrete will have to be cut to length with a pipe cutter. Use a 2-inch pipe cutter, holding the bottom of the post with a pipe wrench to keep it from spinning in the concrete.

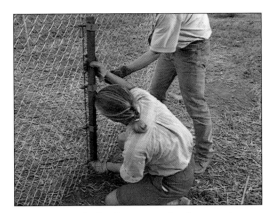

7 *To stretch the fence mesh*, slip a tension bar into the mesh a few feet from the end post. Hook one end of a come-along winch to the tension bar, and the other end to the post.

8 *Winch the fabric* until it is tight. You'll know the tension is right when the fencing pops up about 1/2 inch above the top rail. Then give the come-along an additional pull or two.

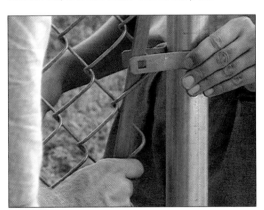

9 *Cut or separate* the fencing so it ends right at the post. Slip a tension bar into the mesh and attach it to the tension bands with carriage bolts.

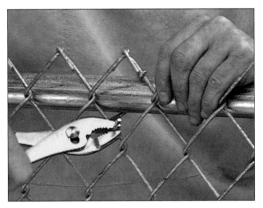

10 *Release the winch,* then tie off the fence with wire ties every 18 inches along the top rail. Then twist four ties onto every intermediate post. You'll need new pliers with good bite to twist the ties.

11 *Gate hardware* consists of two male hinges attached to one post. Carriage bolts secure these firmly. To prevent the gate from being lifted off, hang the top hinge so it points down.

12 *Attach the female section* of the hardware to the gate. Set the gate in place and align it. Once it's positioned, tighten the bolts and attach the latch mechanism.

Lengthening and shortening the mesh

Fencing mesh comes in standard 50-feet rolls. If your fence sections are longer, you'll have to weave sections together at the knuckles. A knuckle is simply the place at the top and bottom where two mesh wires hook together. You bend open the knuckles with pliers until the strand of wire is free, then corkscrew it out with a spiraling action. Use this strand to join the first section of fence to the second section. You may have to unwind a second strand before the mesh fits perfectly together.

Trellis

Y ou can make a trellis in almost any pattern you like, using 1x2 lumber. The basic strategy is to cut and join the perimeter, then fill in the center.

Make two-piece joints with two 2-inch galvanized siding nails; use 2½-inch nails for three-piece joints. The points of the nails will protrude on the back side, so flip the trellis over and clench them (bend them over) with the hammer. To install the trellis, set the trellis legs in post holes. Alternatively, drive two 3-foot pressure-treated stakes into the ground, leaving about 6 inches sticking out of the soil. Fasten the trellis to the stakes with galvanized screws.

Vines for trellises

Train a vine by winding its outside branches around the outer edges of the trellis. The inside branches generally get the idea on their own and will fill in the available space; use twist-ties or string to make them go where you want. Once the vine has a good grip, prune back all the branches you don't want.

Annual vines, like morning glory, must be replanted each spring, perhaps leaving the trellis bare for too much of the season. Perennials, like roses, honeysuckle, and clematis, make an earlier start. Avoid sucker vines, such as Boston ivy, which can overpower and destroy a simple wooden trellis.

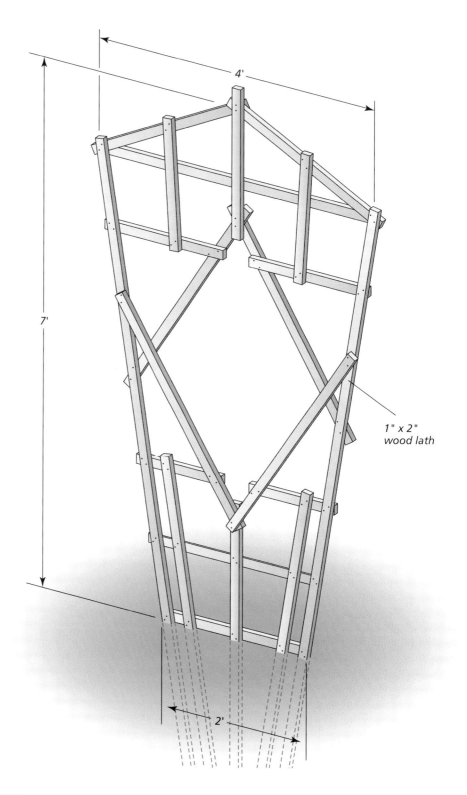

4'

7'

1" x 2" wood lath

2'

Gateway Arbor

If you can build a fence, you can build an arbor like this. Make the side panels first, connecting the 4x4 posts with pairs of 2x4 rails. The arch shown here can be cut from a single 2x12. For a wider arbor, you'll have to miter together two or three pieces of wood to make the arch.

Fasten the arch assembly to the top of the posts with galvanized screws. Attach temporary braces to maintain the post spacing, then set the posts in the ground. Check that the structure is plumb and level, and anchor the posts in gravel or concrete. Then remove the braces and hang the gate.

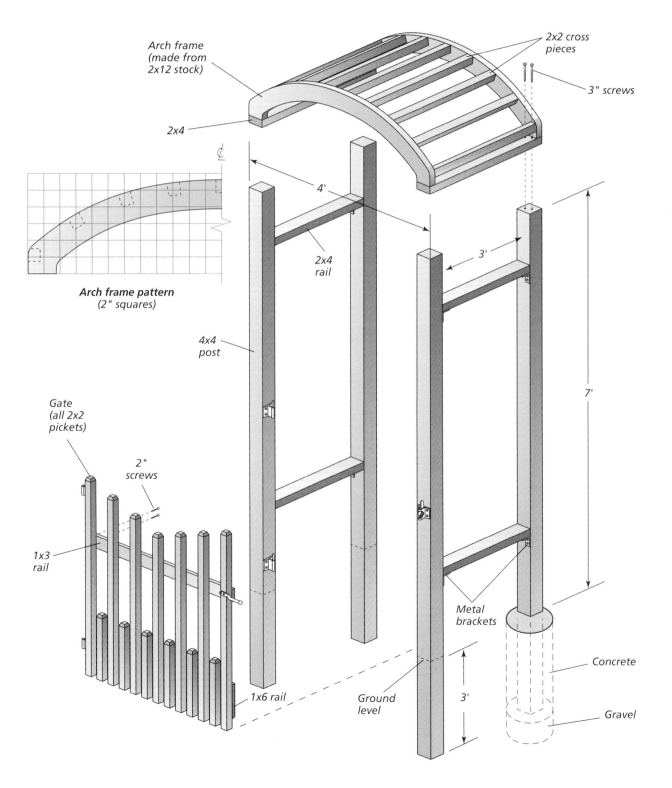

Arch frame (made from 2x12 stock)

2x4

Arch frame pattern (2" squares)

2x2 cross pieces

3" screws

4'

2x4 rail

3'

7'

4x4 post

Gate (all 2x2 pickets)

2" screws

1x3 rail

1x6 rail

Metal brackets

Ground level

3'

Concrete

Gravel

Shade Arbor

This shade arbor can be built to almost any size. It's robust enough to support grape vines, whose leaves will make dense shade. The bench is not structural, so you can omit it if you like.

To build the arbor, set the posts in the ground. After the concrete cures, bolt the cross-beams to the posts, then toenail the rafters across the cross-beams. Nail or screw the cross-rails between the posts. Build the bench seats on the rails, setting their front legs into the ground for extra stability. Make the bench back as a separate assembly, then screw it to the posts and cross-rails.

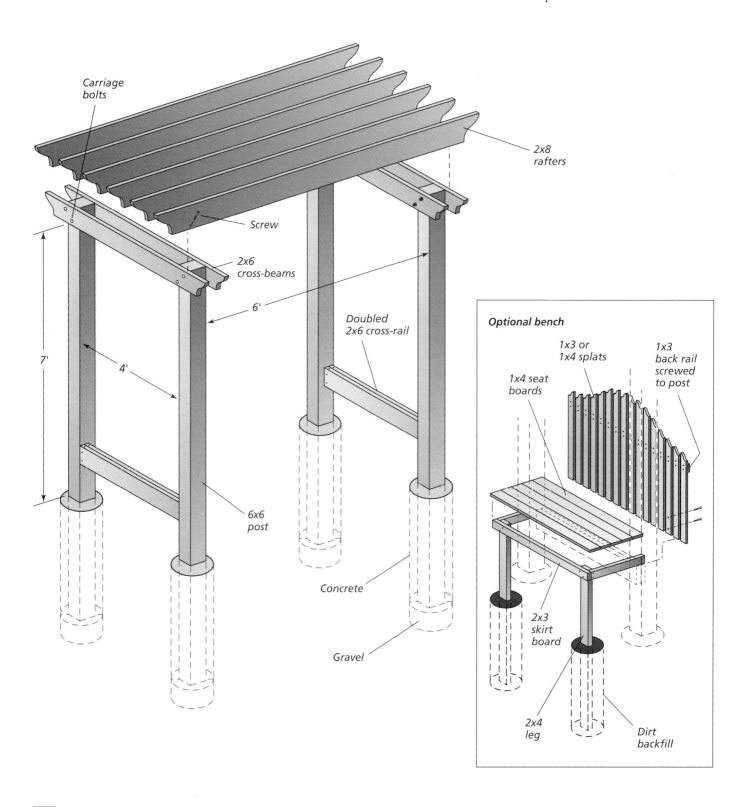

Carriage bolts

2x8 rafters

Screw

2x6 cross-beams

6'

7'

4'

Doubled 2x6 cross-rail

6x6 post

Concrete

Gravel

Optional bench

1x3 or 1x4 splats

1x3 back rail screwed to post

1x4 seat boards

2x3 skirt board

2x4 leg

Dirt backfill

WATER

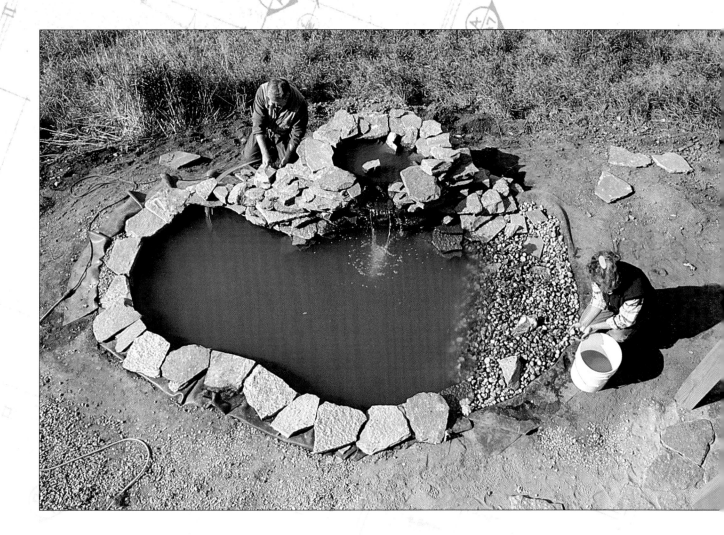

Even during the years when rainfall is generous*, most gardeners face at least a few dry spells. To keep shrubs, flowers, and vegetables healthy, you can either drag sprinklers around your property, or stand at the end of a hose for what seems like hours. Or you could install a drip irrigation system, and let it do all that time-consuming work.*

You can also make water into a landscaping element by building a pond. Ponds are surprisingly easy to install, and give you the opportunity to grow unusual plants, raise fish and other aquatic life, and enjoy the birds that come to drink.

Low-Flow Drip Irrigation

Low-flow drip irrigation systems offer an affordable, environmentally sensible solution to the problem of watering your landscape.

The basic system consists of one or more header tubes attached to the faucet, with feeder tubes branching off to various beds and individual plants. There's usually a back-flow preventer or anti-siphon valve at the faucet itself, plus a pressure regulator to hold the water pressure down to about 30 PSI. This is what allows it to drip instead of spray. A removable end-cap on each header allows it to be cleaned out and drained. Before it goes into service, a new system should be flushed out at full pressure.

The major fittings of most drip systems thread together like garden hose. The feeder lines usually push into T-fittings, which can branch as often as necessary. Although you probably could plug parts from different sys-

1 *The anti-siphon valve* attached to the faucet prevents a clogged system from backing up into the house water supply. In most places, this will be required by the building code. A pressure regulator reduces the faucet water pressure for drip irrigation.

2 *Connect soaker hoses* to the poly pipe with push-together T-fittings. Make sure they're clean and fully seated or else you'll have leaks.

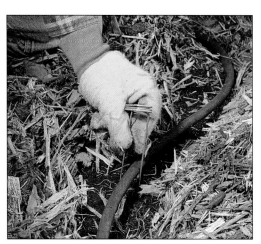

3 *Push wire staples* over the hose to keep it in place. Don't make a staple so tight that it interferes with the water flow.

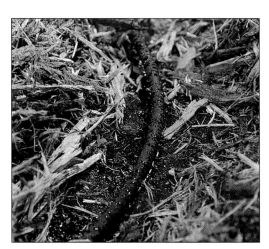

4 *The soaker hose* slowly leaks water all along its length.

tems together, different brands may use water at different rates: you'll avoid problems by sticking with one manufacturer. The product literature will tell you how many devices can be attached to each header tube.

A variety of watering devices can be attached to the feeder tubes. Soaker hoses weep water along their entire length, so they're good for watering an entire bed. Freezing won't harm them, so they're popular in northern climates. Drip emitters and micro-sprinklers deliver water to individual plants.

They're made with a variety of flow rates to accommodate the needs of different plants. Since these fittings shouldn't be allowed to freeze, in cold climates they either have to be taken up before winter, or drained and blown out with compressed air. In any climate, it's a good idea to remove the end caps and flush the system every year.

While it's possible to load a drip system with expensive timers and controls, most people don't bother. Usually you can just turn the system on for part of the day.

1 *Drip fittings connect* ¼-inch drip tubing (or ¼-inch soaker hose) to the ½-inch poly pipe. *Attach a length of tubing for each drip emitter and micro sprinkler.*

2 *Attach a drip emitter* or micro sprinkler to the other end of the tubing. Whichever *device you choose, position it to put water exactly where your plants need it.*

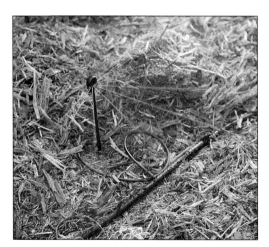

3 *Low-volume micro sprinklers* disperse water over ground covers and other closely *spaced plantings. This one has six spray patterns and an adjustable spray distance.*

4 *Drip emitters supply* water to the base of each plant. Their flow rates range from ½ *gallon to 4 gallons per hour. Choose the type and number of drippers for each plant based on its water requirements.*

Building a Water Garden

The way to create a custom shaped water garden is with a flexible pond liner made of plastic or rubber. Flexible liners lend themselves to the irregular shapes that look most natural in a garden setting. There are two types of liner materials: PVC plastic and synthetic EPDM rubber. PVC doesn't last as long as EPDM, but it is cheaper. Whatever material you choose, go for the thickest liner you can afford.

How deep?

The bigger the pond, the deeper it should be. Big, shallow ponds tend to have algae problems and the water can become too warm to support some forms of aquatic life. The minimum depth for raising plants and small fish is between 15 and 18 inches; larger ponds (with a surface area of between 100 and 200 square feet) should be at least 24 inches deep. If you'll be raising the colorful Oriental carp called koi, which can grow quite large, your pond needs to be 4 feet deep.

Where to build a water garden

Most aquatic plants flourish in full sun, so try to site your pond where it will receive sun for most of the day. If you plan to raise fish, though, you'll need to provide some shade during the hottest hours. Although large trees may seem like logical shade-makers, they make poor pond neighbors. Their root systems eventually will penetrate pond walls, causing major damage, and falling leaves and needles will quickly muck up the water.

1 *Level the top edges* of the excavation. If you don't, the liner will always be visible on the high side. A water level is one way to take readings around the perimeter of the excavation.

2 **Lay out the pond** with a garden hose, then dig down 2 inches farther than the final depth. Make the sides slope about 20 degrees. Dig steps for marginal (shallow-water) plants.

3 **Remove all rocks** and debris that could puncture the liner, then shovel in a 2-inch-thick layer of vermiculite or damp sand to cushion the liner and protect it from any sharp rocks or roots that heave to the surface during cold winters. Cover the walls and bottom with a ¼-inch pad of wet newspaper.

4 **Drape the liner** over the pond and smooth the wrinkles out of it. Leave a healthy overlap of at least 18 inches around the perimeter.

5 **Run water** into the pond and let its weight help you smooth the liner. Get inside the pond and push the liner into the corners and edges. Make careful tucks in the corners.

Water safety

Water is as attractive to children as it is dangerous. Never underestimate the quantity of water in which a child can drown. Most communities require that ponds deeper than 18 inches be fenced to keep out both your own and the neighborhood kids, and your homeowner's insurance may also impose fencing requirements.

6 **Weight the top edge** of the liner with a layer of coping stones. Use sharp scissors to trim the liner about 6 inches beyond the stones.

7 **Fold** the liner onto the coping stones and cover the edge with a second layer of stone. When the pond is full, the water will come halfway up the bottom stone.

Hooking up the electricals

Pumps, filters, and the lights that softly illuminate the waterscape at night all need electricity to run. Some pumps come with a waterproof cord that simply plugs into a GFCI receptacle on the side of your house. If your pump/filtration/lighting system is more complex, or if the cord doesn't reach your pond, you'll have to install a separate weathertight outlet box with a GFCI receptacle near the pond. Then run waterproof underground cable from the box to the house through in an 18-inch deep trench; local code may also require you to put the buried cable inside PVC conduit. Don't skimp on the depth of the trench or you risk nicking the cable with a gardening tool. Place a few markers along the cable's path to refresh your memory later on. Low-voltage (12-volt) lighting is inexpensive and easy to install.

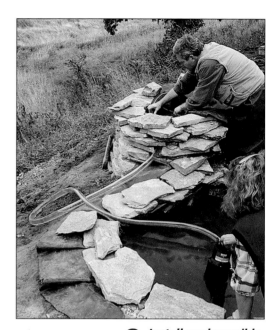

8 *Install a submersible pump* to filter the water. The same pump can also create a waterfall. Run the plastic tubing through the rocks and along the ground, where it will be hidden by plants.

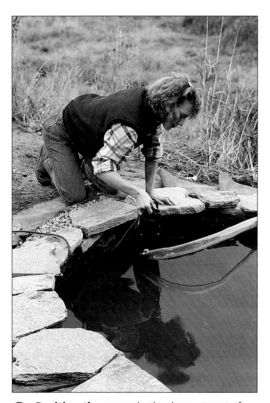

9 *Position the pump* in the deepest part of the pond and as close to the waterfall as possible. Select a pump that can circulate the entire volume of water once an hour, more if there is a waterfall.

10 *Make* a shallow basin at the top of the waterfall, and weight the inlet hose with rocks. Arrange the rocks to make a lip, or weir, where the water can flow out of the basin.

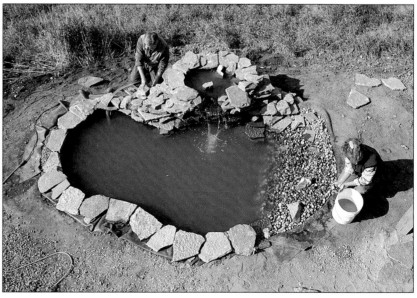

11 *Create natural looking* rock formations to cover the liner and hoses. If you make a pebble beach, rinse the stones first to keep debris out of the water.

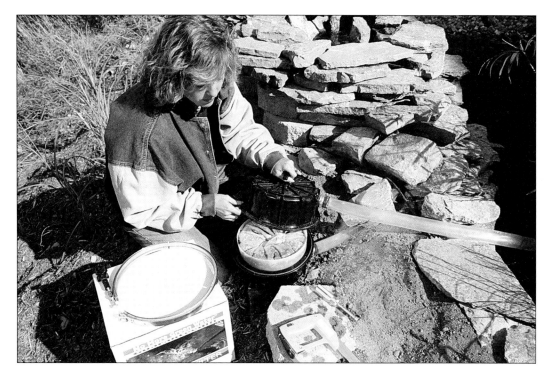

12 *A pressurized canister filter* goes between the pond and the waterfall. The incoming water enters at the top, then the pump pushes the water through the filter, which must be cleaned about once a week.

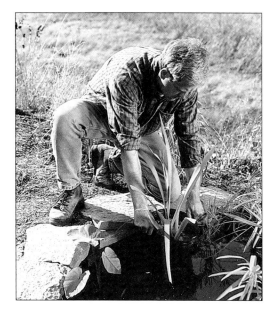

14 *The depth at which you sink* a plant depends on its type. If your pond doesn't have a ledge for shallow-water plants, set them on over-turned containers.

13 *Invasive aquatic plants* are usually planted in submerged plastic containers. Use heavy garden soil with a layer of gravel on top. Rinse the pot and gravel to keep loose soil from muddying the water.

15 *To acclimate* fish, leave them in the plastic bag and float it in the pond for an hour before releasing them. Provide places to hide from raccoons and birds by sinking large rocks and pieces of drain tile in the water.

Installing a rigid pond liner

There are two alternatives to making ponds with flexible liners: preformed plastic shells and concrete.

Preformed shells are best for small ponds. You still have to excavate, but once the hole is dug, installation is a snap. Shells are made of either preformed fiberglass or molded-plastic, they're almost puncture-proof, and they come in a variety of free-form shapes. Durability has a direct relationship to wall thickness – and to price.

Concrete is the traditional material of pond-making, though it's been almost entirely supplanted by liners. While a properly installed concrete pond is permanent, it's labor intensive and expensive. In addition, if the concrete cracks as it settles or during an ice-up, you're stuck – repairs are nearly impossible. In fact, the typical solution is to drain the pond and cover the concrete with a liner.

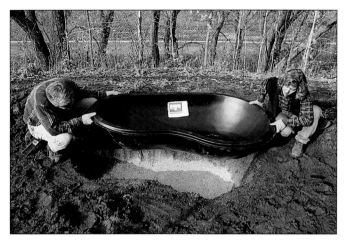

1 *Dig the hole* about 2 inches wider and deeper than the shell. *If your shell has a built-in shelf for plants, dig out a ledge in the soil to support it. Make sure the top edge of the liner ends up level.*

2 *Slowly fill the shell* and as it fills, backfill the walls with *vermiculite or damp sand. Tamp the sand and soil as you go, so it supports the liner firmly and uniformly.*

3 *Set coping stones* around the rim of the pond to disguise *the edge and help blend the pond naturally into its surroundings. The stones should overlap the shell edge by about 2 inches.*

What about winter?

If you live in a moderate climate with little or no frost, not much needs to be done to prep the water garden for winter, except keeping the water free of fallen leaves.

In areas with more severe winters, hardy lilies and marginal plants can safely over-winter, provided the pond doesn't freeze solid. Since fish enter a state of semi-hibernation during the winter, they can stay, too, if a small section stays free of ice so oxygen can enter the water. Either run the pump for several hours a day, or install a pond deicer.

OUTDOOR LIGHTING

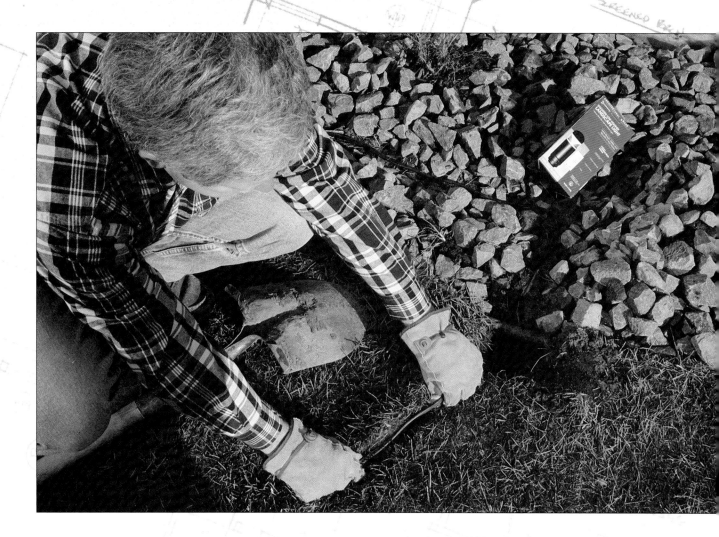

Outdoor lighting makes walkways safe for evening strolling, and it enhances security by depriving prowlers of places to lurk. Good lighting also highlights interesting features and leaves unattractive ones hidden in the dark. The fundamental decision is whether to install regular 110-volt lighting, or a stepped-down 12-volt system. The 110-volt system can produce much higher levels of illumination. However, the installation must proceed strictly according to code, so it may require getting a permit and hiring an electrician. As a result, the 110-volt system can be expensive. Low-voltage lighting systems, on the other hand, are versatile, safe, and inexpensive. What's more, you can install them yourself.

Planning

It's important to plan the complete outdoor lighting system before you install any cables and fixtures. One way to do this is to spend several evenings outdoors, experimenting with flashlights and battery-powered lanterns.

Set your lantern in various positions around a favorite shrub and study the different effects you can create. You'll soon come to understand the difference between spot lighting and flood illumination, between light that shines upward and light that shines downward, and between light that originates behind a tree or shrub and light that originates in front of it. There are no correct answers here – just go with what looks best to you.

More light is not necessarily better. Reserve the brightest lights for steps and walkways. When in doubt, don't rush to more and brighter fixtures. Instead, experiment with where the fixtures are placed; you'll probably find you can create the effect you want.

Don't forget about year-round maintenance when you locate the fixtures. While they can stand being buried under snow, the fixtures won't survive a pass through the snow thrower.

Timers and switches

There are three different ways of controlling outdoor lights: manually, with a timer, and with a photosensitive switch.

A manual switch or set of switches can be mounted at the transformer or inside the house. This allows you to turn the lights on and off whenever you want, but it also requires that you remember to do so.

A timer can be set to turn the lights on and off at the same times every day. The advantage of a timer is constancy: it doesn't forget. One disadvantage is that the timer can't automatically compensate for the season of the year. Plan to reset the timer at the transitions to and from daylight saving time.

A photosensitive switch turns the lights on and off according to the level of ambient light. Some timer-sensor combinations can turn the lights on at sunset and off again after a set number of hours, so they don't remain on until sunrise. The advantage is that you can set the switch and forget it. The disadvantage is that dark clouds, snow, dirt, or insects may trigger the lights to turn on, and light spilling from other light fixtures may trigger the system to turn off.

Lighting plan

As you decide where to put light fixtures, mark their locations on your site drawing. The objective is to create separate lighting circuits, each containing a group of fixtures connected by a single cable. Low-voltage wiring suffers voltage drop on long cable runs, so a long run might not be able to handle as many fixtures as a short one. Most 12-volt transformers can power five or six lights on a single circuit; some transformers can direct power to two, three, or four circuits.

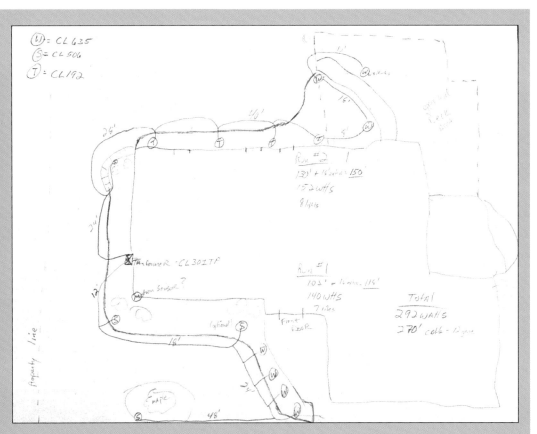

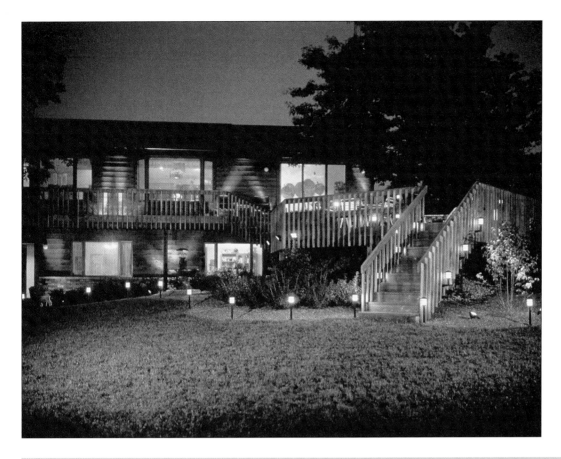

The key to designing outdoor lighting is to forget about replacing the sun, because it can't be done. Instead, use lights for safety, for security, and for accenting the landscape.

Many choices in low-voltage lights

Your final plan should give you enough information to make up a shopping list of fixtures, controls, and cable. You'll have fewest problems if you stick with components from a single product line. You should find what you need at the home center, but if not, consult a lighting dealer.

Low-voltage lights now come in a wide variety of styles. While most of the ones shown here have to be hooked up to a 12-volt power supply, an increasing number are also available as solar-powered units. These are more expensive in the first place, but they are portable, easy to install, can be placed near water, and there's no additional cost for wiring or electricity.

Decorative accent lights are attractive by day and by night. They come in many styles, but may be expensive.

Small flood lights shine upward, creating highlights and shadows. They can be rotated to put light where you want it.

Half-moon walkway lights are unobtrusive, making pathways safe without glare.

Tier lights accent plantings, illuminate walkways, and provide general outdoor brightness.

This solar-powered tier light has silicon cells to soak up energy by day. It's released by a photosensitive trigger at night.

Installation

Low-voltage lighting is easy to install. Start by checking the outlet you'll plug the control box into. The National Electrical Code requires any outdoor outlet to be protected by a ground-fault circuit interrupter (GFCI). This life-saving device instantly shuts off the juice in case of a short to ground. If necessary, replace the existing outlet with a GFCI receptacle before you connect your outdoor lighting equipment.

The lighting circuits can be made with a two-wire cable, which does not require a separate ground wire. While you can string the cable above the ground, it's best to bury it under sod or mulch where it won't be vulnerable to foot traffic, maintenance equipment, and children.

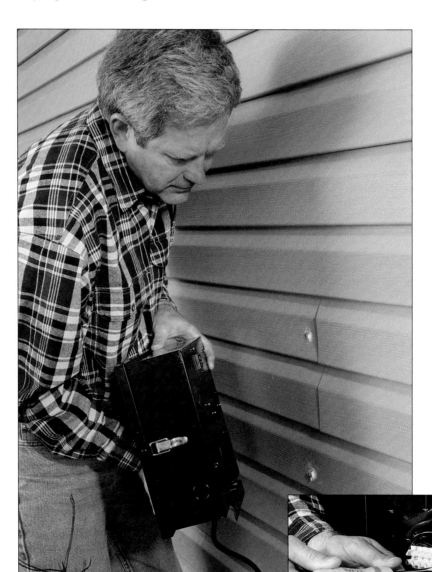

1 *Hang* the lighting control box on screws driven through the siding and into the building's wood framing. Hang the box in a sheltered location (out of direct rain and snow) somewhere near an outdoor electrical outlet.

2 *Connect the wires* to the appropriate terminals. This box accommodates two low-voltage circuits, each having two branches. Note the terminals at right which bring 110-volt power to the transformer.

Each fixture attaches to the cable with a simple snap-on or screw-down connector. Some brands come with connectors attached to wires that leave the fixture, while other brands require you to buy a separate connector for each fixture. Either way, the connection gets made when a little metal spike penetrates the insulation on the cable and contacts the copper wire inside. Since it's possible for the spike to miss the wire, it's best to locate the fixtures, run the cable, and test the circuit before you bury anything. You might also want to run the system through the night so you can tweak the placement of the lights before burying the cable.

Lighting fixtures usually mount on plastic stakes that you push into the ground. However, these stakes don't offer much resistance to weather and ground movement, so you are liable to find yourself repairing and replacing them every year. You can beef them up by making your own wooden stakes. To do this, drive a 2-foot pressure-treated wooden stake into the ground, leaving a couple of inches sticking up. Then push the plastic stake into the ground next to it, and connect the two with a couple of plastic wire ties. If the stake

is unsightly, you can drive it a little deeper, but be careful not to break the plastic fixture.

If there's any chance that rambunctious teenagers or zealous gardeners will drive go-carts, dirt bikes, or garden equipment over the cable, you'll have to do more than rake a little mulch onto it. Use a square spade to open a 6-inch-deep slit in the ground and push the cable down to the bottom. Then fill the slit with dirt or tamp it closed with your foot.

4 **To set the timer**, turn the numbered ring until the arrow lines up with the current time of day. Insert pairs of plastic pins to set the on and off times for the lights.

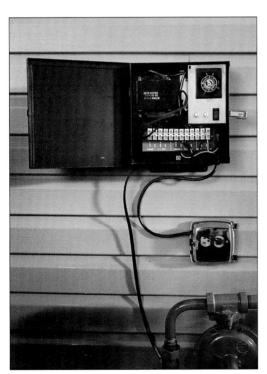

3 **This control box contains** a mechanical timer (top right), a master on-off switch, and two circuit breakers. One low-voltage circuit has been connected and is ready to test.

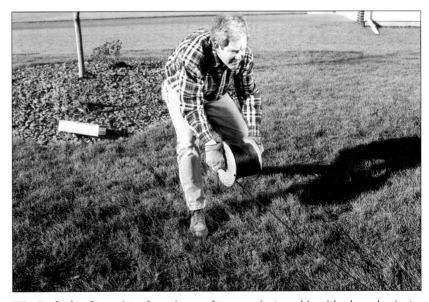

5 **Each circuit** consists of a main run of two-conductor cable with a branch wire to each lighting fixture. Route the cable where it can be buried under sod or hidden under shrubs and mulch.

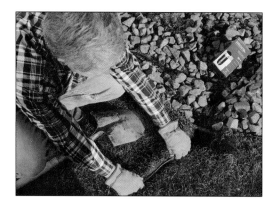

6 *Run* the main cable past each fixture. Slice through the sod to bury the electrical cable; it doesn't have to be deep, but it must be out of the way for mowing. Run the cable under any edging.

8 *Each fixture has two wires* to be connected to the main or branch cable. Some styles snap together, driving a metal spur through the cable insulation. Other styles screw together, with the screw forcing the spur into the cable.

7 *Smear the base* of the bulb with petroleum jelly to prevent corrosion, install the bulb, and put the fixture together according to the manufacturer's instructions.

9 *Always bury the cables* under sod, mulch, or stones. If you leave them exposed, they're certain to be uprooted by yard work or by active children.

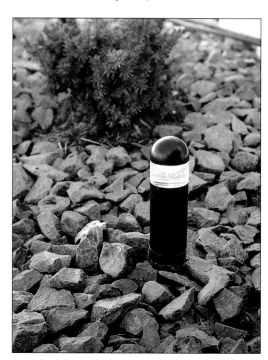

10 *Test the lights* before you bury the cables. Make sure that each lamp comes on, and check it by night to be sure it throws light where you want it.

LAWNS and LAWN ALTERNATIVES

Lush green turf feels good underfoot *and there's nothing better than a nice lawn for play. A healthy swath of green will make your landscape sparkle, enhancing your trees, shrubs, and flowers. However, the larger the lawn, the greater the maintenance it will need. If you're already pressed for time, you may find that mowing, watering, fertilizing, and weeding becomes an endless and burdensome chore. Lawn alternatives such as ground covers, ornamental grasses, and native plantings can produce different effects that require less ongoing labor. These alternatives not only require less maintenance, but also conserve water and reduce the need for pesticides and chemicals.*

Lawns

All lawn grasses fall into one of two basic groups depending on where they grow best. Cool-season grasses typically thrive where there is some snow cover in winter. Warm-season grasses flourish in hot climates where the winters are mild. Within each of these groups are many varieties, including some newer, low-maintenance grasses. You'll have a stronger, healthier lawn if you combine several grasses that are commonly grown in your region. Consult with suppliers to match the characteristics of the grass to the particulars of your soil, sun, and rainfall patterns. Also think about how you'll use the lawn. Areas with heavy foot traffic will require different grasses than lawns planted primarily for show.

Preparing the lawn area

The first step in installing a new lawn is measuring the yard. Break down the lawn area into units of 1,000 square feet because the materials you buy to install and maintain lawns typically are calculated and packaged in quantities for 1,000 square feet.

Soil preparation is the same, no matter which grass types and planting method you choose. Start by removing debris and large soil clods. Break up clumps bigger than a golf ball, but don't pulverize the soil. Spread a fertilizer recommended for new lawns, along with any other amendments called for by your soil tests. Use a mechanical spreader to regulate the spread according to the instructions on the bag. Rototill 4 to 6 inches down to mix the topsoil with the subsoil. This prevents formation of a water barrier between the two layers, which would inhibit root growth.

Grading and rolling

Bring the lawn to finish grade with a garden rake, then remove all stray rocks or debris. Slope the grade away from the house for proper drainage. Get rid of low spots where water might pool and high spots that could get scalped by the mower. When you have a smooth surface, you're ready to compact the soil with a water-filled roller (available from

Starting a new lawn

Sod is the most expensive way to start a new lawn, but it gives you instant results. Seeding is the least expensive method, but it takes the longest time for the lawn to establish. Sprigs, which are pieces of plant stem, and plugs, which are small circles of sod, cost more than seed but less than sod. Sprigs and plugs are most commonly used to establish a lawn with warm-season hybrid plants for which there is no viable seed. With plugs you can expect good cover in two months. Sprigs can take as long as a couple of years to fill in and look lush. Both sprigged and plugged areas must be weeded until coverage is established.

Sod

The best times to lay sod are autumn and early spring. Plan to lay the sod as soon as it's delivered. If you leave it rolled up too long, it may mildew or dry out. Healthy sod won't have brown edges, dried-out patches, or mildew.

Stagger the joints on adjacent strips and press the pieces tightly together as you work. Where you need to cut, use a sharp knife and cut from the soil side.

Once all the sod is down, roll it with a water-filled roller to ensure good contact with the soil. Then water the sod thoroughly. Water daily for the first 7 to 10 days.

Seed

With seed you get what you pay for, so choose high-quality seed with little weed content. Spread starter fertilizer first, then spread the seed according to the application rates specified on the package.

Rake lightly to embed the seed about ¼ inch into the soil. Roll the area with a water-filled roller, then mulch with ¼ inch of straw to keep the seed in place and conserve moisture. Keep the top ¼-inch of the seedbed moist while the seed germinates. Begin by applying small amounts of water several times a day, more often if the weather is hot and dry. As the grass grows, water less often but increase the quantity of water so it penetrates deep into the soil.

rental stores). Fill the roller about ⅓ full and roll the soil until it's firm enough so that you don't see your footprints as you go along. Water the soil just enough to settle it. Don't overdo it or you'll make a muddy mess.

Lawn maintenance

You can expect to fertilize a lawn two times each year. While some people prefer more frequent feedings, remember that the more you fertilize the more you will have to mow. An early spring feeding (given just after the first flush of new growth) gives the lawn a good start for the summer. A fall feeding is important to help the grass through the winter.

Expect to mow frequently during the springtime, less often in summer and fall. In general, mow often enough so you don't remove more than one-third of the leaf. Make sure the mower is sharp, or it will shred and bruise the leaves, increasing the risk of disease. Short clippings from frequent mowings can be allowed to fall without raking. They'll soon decompose, returning nutrients to the soil.

It's best to water grass in the early morning. You won't burn the grass by watering during the heat of the day, but you will lose more water to evaporation. Avoid watering at night, because this encourages mildew and fungal disease. To stay healthy, grass needs between 1 and 2 inches of water per week throughout the growing season, whether from rainfall or by sprinkling. A good soaking is better than frequent light waterings, which encourage the growth of thatch around the base of the plants.

Grass sprigs

Sprigs are small sections of grass stems with the roots attached. You can buy sprigs by the bushel, or you can pull them from sections of sod. To plant sprigs, either scatter them or place them in shallow, evenly spaced furrows. For scattering, you'll need 5 to 8 bushels of sprigs per 1,000 square feet. If you're planting in rows, space zoysia grass sprigs 6 inches apart and bermuda grass sprigs 12 inches apart.

After planting, top-dress the lawn with ½ inch of soil, roll the lawn, then water thoroughly. Water initially to a depth of 4 to 6 inches, then keep the water coming until the plants have developed good root systems.

Grass plugs

Grass plugs usually come in 2- to 4-inch diameter circles, or you can cut your own from rolls of sod using a rented plugging tool. Use the same tool to punch holes for the plugs, or else scoop out the holes with a narrow trowel. Space the plugs about 12 inches apart in a checkerboard pattern.

Drop the plugs into the prepared soil, bringing the soil even with the crown (where the roots meet the leaves). Firm the soil around the roots and water immediately to moisten the soil to the depth of the plugs. About ½ inch of water every other day should be enough for good growth.

Why burn a prairie?

The dramatic fires that occasionally race across natural prairies serve several useful purposes. The flames consume the tall, woody plants that would eventually overshadow and destroy their sun-loving neighbors. The heat of the fire also weakens the seeds of pesky weeds. The blackened earth left by the fire soaks up the sun's heat, encouraging hot-season plants to germinate. While the prairie may look desolate after burning, the root systems of the plants are actually strengthened, causing them to send out new growth. You should occasionally burn a prairie garden, but get permission from the local fire department first.

Tall-grass prairies *typically contain 60% to 90% grasses, along with self-seeding perennials, annuals, and biennials. To establish a prairie, you need well-drained soil and full sun.*

Home Prairies

Prairie gardens and other native plantings, such as high alpine meadows in the mountain states or desert chaparral, are an alternative to expanses of closely cropped lawn. Once established, they don't require weeding, mowing, watering, or fertilizing. But the informal look of native plants isn't suitable for all neighborhoods. Discuss your plans with the owners of adjacent properties. Also check your local regulations, which may define your native plants as undesirable weeds subject to control ordinances.

Getting started

The easiest way to start a prairie or meadow garden is with a seed mixture. Broadcast it over tilled soil and water daily until the seeds

germinate. A prairie garden started from seed will take three or four years to fill in.

If you want quicker results, you can transplant young native wildflowers and prairie or meadow plants, then fill in the spaces with seed. However, transplant from other parts of your own property, or buy plants from local nurseries specializing in native plants – don't go digging in the wilds. In most areas it's illegal to take plants from public lands.

You'll have to weed diligently for the first two or three years to ferret out undesirable – and often invasive – species. After that, the desirable prairie and meadow plants should dominate. If the annuals don't reliably self-seed and you're left with bare or weedy patches, just cultivate those areas and sow fresh annual seed.

Short-grass prairies
and wildflower meadows consist of perennials and self-seeding annuals and biennials, with native grasses mixed in. Wildflower seeds must be sown on well-cultivated soil.

Ground Covers

There are ground covers available for just about every climate, light, and soil condition. Ground covers don't require much maintenance beyond an occasional leaf-blowing and mulching. If the varieties you select grow quickly, you may need to cut them back occasionally.

Plant ground covers in staggered rows, spaced as recommended by the nursery where you buy the plants. Spacing is important – overcrowded plants will soon jam against each other, but plants placed too far apart will take forever to fill in. To plant, re-move the seedlings from the flat and separate them, set them in the ground, tamp the soil around the base of each plant, and water well. A handful of peat moss or composted manure in the hole will help the plant get started. If the roots seem pot-bound, make a few vertical cuts around the rootball to break the circular growth pattern. A 2- to 3-inch layer of mulch will keep weeds down until the plants start to spread, but hold the mulch back from the plant stems to allow air circulation. It's critical to keep the roots of ground covers moist, so plan on watering daily during the first month.

Moss phlox grows from 4 to 6 inches tall. The pink, white, purple, or violet flowers form a thick carpet atop the plant's needle-like leaves.

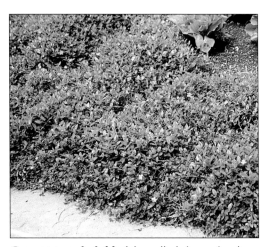

Common periwinkle (also called vinca minor) reaches a height of about 6 inches. It forms a loose carpet of trailing stems, which are covered with lavender-blue blooms in spring.

Deep-rooted wildflowers can help hold the soil on steep slopes, controlling erosion.

Purple Siberian squill spills over the rocks in this northern landscape.

Index